MINNESOTA DRAMA EDITIONS, NO. 6 · EDITED BY STEPHEN PORTER

TWO PLAYS BY CHARLES BERTIN

Christopher Columbus and *Don Juan*

TRANSLATED BY

WILLIAM JAY SMITH

Minneapolis

UNIVERSITY OF MINNESOTA PRESS IN ASSOCIATION WITH THE
MINNESOTA THEATRE COMPANY

CAUTION: These plays are fully protected, in whole, in part, or in any form under the copyright laws of the United States of America, the British Empire including the Dominion of Canada, and all other countries of the Copyright Union, and are subject to royalty. All rights, including professional, amateur, motion picture, radio, television, recitation, public reading, and any method of photographic reproduction, are strictly reserved, and no performance may be made without permission in writing. All inquiries should be addressed to Gilbert Parker, Curtis Brown, Ltd., 60 East 56 Street, New York, New York 10022.

TRANSLATOR'S NOTE

IN BOTH PLAYS my aim has been to keep the language as clean and uncluttered as possible — more difficult by far in *Don Juan* than in *Christopher Columbus* — in order to portray in straightforward contemporary speech, as does the original, passions that speak for all time with elegance and classical simplicity.

The Christian names of some of the characters in *Christopher Columbus* have been anglicized. In *Don Juan* the Marquess de la Mota has become simply Don Manuel La Mota. I have used "Anne," as does M. Bertin, rather than the correct Spanish, "Ana," for "Anne de Ulloa," because it seems both simpler and more appropriate. In *Don Juan* also I have kept, as does the author, forms of address and titles which are, in general, in keeping with the nationalities of the characters.

W. J. S.

TWO PLAYS BY CHARLES BERTIN

INTRODUCTION

by Stephen Porter

THE inclusion of the Belgian playwright Charles Bertin's *Christopher Columbus* and *Don Juan* in what is specifically designated as a director's series oriented toward practical work on the stage may come as a surprise. The American director who picks up a modern play about a great legendary or historical character is almost certainly expecting opportunities for busy stage action and contemporary reinterpretation in the vein of Brecht, or at least a consciously anachronistic wit in the vein of Shaw and Giraudoux, both of whom got extra mileage out of overfamiliar heroes by dosing them with irony, fantasy, and flippancy. M. Bertin will have none of these restoratives. His stagecraft is so austere in what it leaves out that a hasty reader may wonder what, if anything, it leaves in.

It leaves in an eloquence which repeatedly suggests poetry and yet remains, except for the chorus of Columbus's sailors, strictly within the limits of a heightened realistic prose. Concentration, rather than ornamentation, gives the dialogue its luminosity. In the dramatic structure a similar concentration, amounting in *Christopher Columbus* to a deliberate suppression of any hint of external action, injects, I believe, an explosive intensity into the simple mechanics of opening doors or kneeling and rising, and, in the slightly more physicalized *Don Juan*, into such actions as hiding behind a curtain, touching a dagger, and falling on the floor in floods of tears.

Most of us are unprepared for such total subservience of stage action to the word, except in radio drama. It comes as no surprise that the works in this volume were first performed on the air; and a director unacquainted with French theatrical traditions could be pardoned for believing that the air is where they belong. He would be mistaken. Both plays have been successfully produced in Belgium and on tour. They have attracted major actors of the French stage, notably guest artists from the Comédie Française. These people are at home in M. Bertin's austerely simplified structures and know exactly what to do with them. To oversimplify, the plays stem from Racine rather than Shakespeare, and they require, or at any rate reward, the rather special training that an actor undergoes before attempting Racine — an arduous discipline closer to the daily sweat of a dancer or an athlete than to the subjective and often self-indulgent emotionalism of our typical classroom training and rehearsal procedures. Instead of encouraging the idiosyncrasies of what our acting coaches describe as behavior, the Comédie Française and its school, the Conservatoire, train their heroic actors to deny the very existence of their bodies. To illustrate with one perhaps old-fashioned and one very contemporary example: first, Napoleon claimed that no one in tragedy should ever sit down, because the flexing of the joints was mechanical and therefore intrinsically untragic; second, in Racine performances I have seen the older actors flatten their thumbs across their palms in what could only be an arthritic condition in real life but on stage is considered to be an ennoblement of gesture. A free-flapping thumb, apparently, is beneath the dignity of tragedy.

This suppression of bodily spontaneity is counterbalanced by an enormous expansion of vocal flexibility. Jean-Louis Barrault writes that to play Racine an actor must be able to speak twelve alexandrine lines, 144 syllables, on a single breath, constantly rising in volume and intensity. Young actors aspiring to play tragedy are turned away from school if their rib cages aren't big enough. Tragedians must inherit deep chests just as basketball players must inherit long legs. And then they must practice every day, like singers, if they are not to lose breath in old age.

This high degree of specialization has been until recently a problem for actors who train for the classics but don't want to be cut off from the contemporary stage. In France as in America there has been a tendency to brand an actor as classical or modern and to be excessively critical of him if he pops out of his pigeonhole and tries to change his style. Fortunately there has been an upsurge of modern heroic drama beginning early in this century and reaching its climax in the 1940s and 1950s. *Don Juan*, first broadcast in 1947 with an illustrious cast including Marcel Herrand, Maria Casarès, Jean Davy, Hélène Perdrière, Lucien Nat, and Béatrice Bretty, and *Christopher Columbus*, winner in 1953 of the international Prix Italia for distinction in radio drama, are prominent achievements in this renaissance of eloquence and tragic scale.

The movement began, perhaps, with the stage productions of the early plays of Paul Claudel, who, so it seems, never initially intended them to be performed. In such eventually popular but difficult works as *L'Otage* and *Partage de Midi*, overt action is confined to one burst of violence at the end of three hours of very long poetic arias by very small casts of characters concerned with

5

very obscure points of metaphysical anguish. Claudel, a career diplomat rather than a commercial playwright, understandably did not expect his demands to be met by actors or audiences. Surprisingly, both actors and audiences have risen to the challenge with an enthusiasm which has opened the door for a whole generation of rhetorical writers on intellectual themes. Perhaps the closest to Bertin, both in the eloquence of his prose and in his preference for the harsh moral struggles of Renaissance Spain, is Henry de Montherlant, known to American audiences only through rather shaky productions of *Queen after Death* and *Port-Royal* but commandingly successful in great productions by the major theaters of France. In *The Master of Santiago* and *The Cardinal of Spain* Montherlant creates the same atmosphere of arrogance, of spiritual loneliness, of yearning for and rebellion against God that informs the two plays in this volume, and he employs the same economy of means.

To sum up: those aspects of Bertin's craft which might seem untheatrical to a practicing actor or director ignorant of the French stage are in fact solidly adjusted to the style of major companies of the 1950s and to the taste of their audiences.

Having disposed, or so we hope, of the problems of structure and style, we face a question in the matter of content. The stories have been told before. Previous Don Juans are too numerous and too famous to mention. Columbus has received a rather black comic treatment by Bertin's compatriot Michel de Ghelderode, and Claudel, reversing his earlier practice of subordinating all action to the word, created with the help of Jean-Louis Barrault a *Christophe Colombe* which was a veritable orgy of mixed media: mime; oratorio; scenes simultaneously acted on stage and projected, many times enlarged, on a movie screen disguised as a ship's sail; and a jigging minstrel show of Aztec gods who conspired to prevent Christianity from reaching Mexico by shaking a rope, symbolic of waves, in front of the *Santa Maria*. Faced with all this competition, how does Bertin justify retelling these many-times-told tales?

He does so by giving us the opposite of what we expect. Don Juan, who we feel sure will be a sensualist living for pleasure, is here shown as lonely and desolate because he cannot derive any real pleasure from his conquests. Cursed with a nature that cannot love or suffer through another person, he seems jealous of his masochistically tenacious mistress's ability to feel pain. Unable to want a woman who has surrendered to him, he places his only hope in a girl who resists him and thereby seems to be able to inspire love, but force of habit and an all-too-expert technique of seduction reduce his one potential love to the level of just another conquest. He stands defiantly before God, damned not by his love of pleasure but by his resentment of a deity who created him wrong.

Columbus, who is surely among the least stationary heroes of history, is here presented in a play so deliberately static as to induce claustrophobia. All action is confined to waiting, grumbling, and not quite rebelling in the cabin of the *Santa Maria*, and to lyrically lamenting the sense of isolation in poetic interludes on the deck. Columbus has already reached his peak of resolution or stubbornness before the play begins, and now he can only wait to be proved right. The author's courageous intent is to make us endure the boredom of the voyage as the sailors were forced to endure it — virtually without relief. The success this play has enjoyed on radio and stage is a tribute to the honesty and eloquence with which he has carried out his stark, self-denying plan.

Both plays are fine examples of a school of writing which has done much to vary and enrich French-speaking theater in our century but which remains comparatively unknown to the Anglo-American stage. William Jay Smith's translations will, we hope, help to dispel this ignorance and incite our theaters to experiment with this form of modern high tragedy.

7

CHARLES BERTIN

CHRISTOPHER COLUMBUS

translated by William Jay Smith

Foreword

THIS work, which attempts to recreate the complex, exemplary figure of Christopher Columbus, has for its single setting the *Santa Maria*. The action takes place during Columbus's first voyage, between September 6, 1492, the date of his departure from the Canary Islands, and October 11, the day of his discovery.

This brief period constitutes the peak of Columbus's life. He had prepared himself for twenty years to become the man he was during these few weeks; it is, therefore, not straying from the truth to reduce his countenance to the lineaments it assumed in the course of this trip.

On board the ship itself, the action unfolds in two places against two alternating backgrounds: the Admiral's cabin (the place of the dramatic action) and that part of the deck on which the sailors usually assemble when off duty (the place of the poetic action).

This constant alternation between poetic and dramatic scenes gives the play its meaning.

The scenes on deck attempt to give voice to the conscience of Columbus's crew, and form, in counterpoint to the main action, a sort of poetic commentary, whose lyric tone contrasts with the realism of the speeches in the cabins. I must point out in passing that the divisions I have made in the text between the different voices and the chorus is purely suggestive, and that the director is free to adopt any other he wishes.

The chorus, which does not take part in the action, is witness to it, and, as in classical tragedy, constitutes an emanation of the collective consciousness overwhelmed by great events.

Indeed, the drama of Columbus, which is above all a spiritual adventure, can only stand out properly in relief against the drama of these simple men, for whom the expedition they have undertaken is but an adventure in space.

The scenes on deck serve still another purpose. Alternating from the beginning to the end of the work with the cabin scenes, they communicate to the audience the sense of time passing — passing slowly. Between the opening dialogue, at the time of the departure, and the scene of the discovery, with which the play concludes, five long weeks go by: the audience must, like the actors of the drama, feel their full weight.

The cabin scenes bring Christopher Columbus face to face with his temptations, which have only one aim: to bring him to a failure which could be the failure of his life itself.

These temptations are of three sorts:

1. *Material* temptation: the officers and the crew who struggle against Columbus for their material possessions and their lives;

2. *Spiritual* temptation: the Chaplain, who opposes the explor-

10

er's dangerous experiment with the authority of the all-powerful Church that he represents;

3. *Sentimental* temptation: Alonzo, Columbus's first mate and disciple, whom the Admiral had dreamed of making his successor and who, under the influence of the Chaplain, abandons his master.

The play tells of Columbus's struggles against his tempters and his triumph over them.

But this triumph is that of a single man, for the greatest moment of his life is also his most solitary one. He confronts his success at a time when he has no happiness left within him to greet it. He has rid himself of it along the way, he has repudiated all that was alien to his plan, he has been pruned, like that branch in the Scripture that is pruned so that it may bear more fruit:

"All my life, Vincent, is in this moment . . . If it does not exist, then I have not existed! If this light were suddenly to go out, then God has mocked me! But it shines, Vincent, it shines! And Columbus is finally face to face with Columbus. Face to face with Columbus the wretched, the baffled, beaten madman, for one moment now stands Columbus, the man of God. And you would have me miss that confrontation?"

At the turning point of history, Christopher Columbus, the discoverer, stands out, against the declining Middle Ages, the first spokesman of the modern era . . .

C. B.

CHARACTERS

Arenas   Christopher Columbus
Vincent Pinzón   Pedro Niño
Martin Pinzón   Bartholomew Roldán
Alonzo   Sancho Ruiz

Chorus of sailors

Act I

Dawn, September 6, 1492. The deck of the Santa Maria, *the flagship of Columbus, at anchor off the Canary Islands. A mast, a part of the railing, an open hatchway, rigging . . . Crewmen scattered about, some standing, others seated or lying down, all motionless. One of them strums a guitar. Almost total darkness. On a heap of rope, a lantern gives only a weak light. The light that from time to time illuminates the sky with a brief red flash is from the volcano of Tenerife, which is erupting.*

A VOICE.
　Be still, guitar! Sleep, and let us sleep!
CHORUS.
　Sleep?
　Who speaks of sleeping?
　Has he who speaks of sleeping
　neither guts nor memory?
SECOND VOICE.
　Thirty-four days! Already thirty-four days since we left Palos!
THIRD VOICE.
　Thirty-four days to reach the hellhole they call the Islands of the
　　Blest.
FOURTH VOICE.
　Thirty-four days, thirty-four nights!
CHORUS.
　Sleeper, do you hear?

Do you hear what they are saying?
It is no longer the ocean that rocks the ship at night,
it is the long sweep of anxiety . . .

SECOND VOICE.

Even that volcano signals our unfortunate arrival!

CHORUS.

To whom shall we speak of our hesitation, our perplexity,
we who are the prey to events
and not their guide?
In whom shall we confide our anguish
at this precise point on the earth
to which the whim of the Queen and the will of Columbus
have brought us?

FOURTH VOICE.

In Palos, the year had been bad . . .

SECOND VOICE.

Burning and arid, without a whiff of wind, without a drop of water.

THIRD VOICE.

Not even the hum of a bee's wing nor the breath of a bird!

SECOND VOICE.

Nothing but the leaden slack of the sea beneath the blinding mouth
of the sun . . .

THIRD VOICE.

Nothing, on the deserted fields, but the scars of dead streams and
the white harvests of dust!

CHORUS.

Silence hung on the world like the great scratching of an insect in
a crackling of light.
Animals died beside men. Even wild animals obeyed this strange
call.
Beside bone-dry streams we came upon the hyena and the ox, the
ass and the mountain wolf in a strange brotherly embrace.
God had abandoned us: he had made us his quarry, sweeping in
great circles over our heads, like the hawk over the sheep!
Men touched their foreheads to the dust, women fled, crossing
themselves, into the depths of the houses.

14

O terrible time! No water for the old, no milk for the young! Few lemons and no oranges, few fish, no grapes!

FOURTH VOICE.

Yes, heaven conspired with Columbus in his mad scheme to travel so far!

SECOND VOICE.

Whispering to us that the sea knows no season, but puts profit in your hand!

THIRD VOICE.

He went from place to place, pitying some, flattering others, paying for drinks in the inns . . .

FOURTH VOICE.

On his lips Cipango and Cathay, and all sorts of other exotic names with which he mingled that of the Blessed Virgin . . .

SECOND VOICE.

Sometimes as sly as a vendor selling his shoddy goods with the help of insinuating gestures . . .

THIRD VOICE.

Sometimes as proud as a Jew, with that odd look in his eye when he speaks of the Jerusalem that beckons to him.

CHORUS.

It was too much for us: the choice was not possible!

We chose the less uncertain . . .

settled for the profitable,

locked up our barns, drew in our nets on the sand . . .

Between death at home and fortune abroad,

between the empty stable and his promises,

we chose — oh, in spite of ourselves — to come to this place,

where God has traced the frontier of our domain and the limit of our law:

this imperceptible line on the sea beyond which no one knows what exists.

We came this far with great struggle and great fright.

To what end? We know and we do not know.

We who are balanced between sky and water, between one world and the other,

15

between night that ends
and a new day,
between our fear and the explorer's will.
To what end? We know and we do not know.
We are taken like fish
in a seine,
like birds in a net,
with no defense, no power, and even no will.
How heavy is the night!
The lamp is lighted in the Admiral's cabin . . .
And Providence, the sister of God, shapes great events.
Darkness. Slight strumming of the guitar. The second tableau follows immediately.

SECOND TABLEAU

Columbus's cabin. Simple furnishings. A table with a few books and two large logbooks. Maps. Three chairs. A large crucifix. An hourglass. A low, narrow bed. Two portholes, one opening on the deck and the other on the sea. Just before dawn. From time to time through the porthole can be seen the brief activity of the volcano.

Scene I

As the curtain goes up, Arenas appears at the door.

ARENAS. Are you alone?

VINCENT PINZÓN. We have been awaiting the Admiral, Father. For almost an hour . . . Do you want to see him?

ARENAS. He asked me to attend his meeting with you. I'm surprised not to find him here.

VINCENT PINZÓN. I don't think he has yet returned aboard. His boat took him ashore last night . . .

ARENAS. Alone?

VINCENT PINZÓN. Alonzo was with him.

ARENAS. Strange that he should take so long.

MARTIN PINZÓN. You're very solicitous, Father! The truth is that the captains of his ships are for the Admiral people of very little importance, people it's only fit to keep waiting!

ARENAS. What bitterness, Captain Pinzón! . . .

MARTIN PINZÓN. I'm sorry, but this waiting is getting on my nerves! We've been immobilized here for weeks, in this nasty port, for no reason whatever!

VINCENT PINZÓN. "For no reason whatever" is going a bit far, brother! Especially coming from you . . . I believe it's to your ship that we owe this little stop . . .

MARTIN PINZÓN. An insignificant repair job that the least little shipwright in Spain would have completed in forty-eight hours!

VINCENT PINZÓN. Hm! . . . I saw that rudder. It was split right through. In a rather strange, and somewhat puzzling, way . . .

MARTIN PINZÓN. (*curtly*) Enough of that.

VINCENT PINZÓN. As you wish . . . (*A pause. Turning to Arenas, who has gone to the porthole*) You are watching for him, Father?

ARENAS. I am watching the volcano hurl its flames into the water.

VINCENT PINZÓN. (*approaching*) A pretty spectacle indeed . . .

ARENAS. The ocean is lit up with it for miles around.

MARTIN PINZÓN. The islanders say . . .

VINCENT PINZÓN. You're going to tell us of some catastrophe.

MARTIN PINZÓN. Don't laugh! At the time of the last eruption, twelve years ago, the two ships that were anchored here never returned to port . . .

VINCENT PINZÓN. You really believe in these warnings, brother?

MARTIN PINZÓN. Our crews believe in them, and every day of inactivity makes them worry all the more!

VINCENT PINZÓN. Then on your ship issue orders like those I give on the *Niña*: have the men swab down the decks three times a day! You'll see that a little cleanliness discourages useless dreaming . . .

MARTIN PINZÓN. How you simplify everything! The truth is that our men are afraid, and not just of this volcano.

17

VINCENT PINZÓN. I know, but I also know that you give them reason to fear when nothing, for the moment, justifies their fear. That's what I can't approve of!

MARTIN PINZÓN. You have changed your mind . . .

VINCENT PINZÓN. No!

ARENAS. (*interrupting*) Gentlemen, if I may interrupt . . . I'd like to know exactly what you think.

MARTIN PINZÓN. I want to return to Spain right away, Father.

ARENAS. You really believe that our expedition terminates with this stop in the Canaries?

MARTIN PINZÓN. It proves at least that a long trip is impossible! The breaking of this rudder is a trifle . . . But, tomorrow, there will be something worse! Our boats are old, Father. They are too small, badly equipped, badly stocked, badly commanded. And it is these ships, as shot through with holes as a honeycomb, that an incompetent leader, commanding crews trembling with fear, plans to take across an ocean, about which we know nothing — not even whether or not it has an end!

ARENAS. You seem to have great contempt for the Admiral's scientific prowess . . .

MARTIN PINZÓN. The Admiral's scientific prowess? And where would he have acquired it? In the antechambers of the court? We know only one sure thing about him — that he has asked for much and obtained much. But I am waiting for him to give some proof of his scientific knowledge.

VINCENT PINZÓN. In that case, let him at least have the opportunity to test it, brother.

MARTIN PINZÓN. You have suddenly acquired a taste for heroism?

VINCENT PINZÓN. Let's say rather that I simply have no desire to disgrace myself . . . It is possible that deep within me I believe as little as you in the success of this undertaking . . . But — it's perhaps a weakness on my part — I would judge it unworthy of myself, of you, of our name, and of the honor of these ships, to abandon an expedition that no real danger has yet threatened . . .

MARTIN PINZÓN. These noble sentiments are of very recent date. Several days ago . . .

VINCENT PINZÓN. (*interrupting him*) I love Spain as much as you. Some nights, I must confess, the wind swells with a scent of grass and lilies that takes me by the throat . . . Those nights I feel ready to follow you. And what I told you last week, and what you now hold against me, I shall undoubtedly say to you again . . . But I shall deny it the next day.

MARTIN PINZÓN. (*ironically*) In other words, you are arranging everything so as not to be on anybody's side . . .

VINCENT PINZÓN. (*softly*) I am on the side of my own sincerity. (*a pause*) And, to be absolutely honest, on the side of my curiosity. Yes, I have a great deal of curiosity with respect to this undertaking. It seems to me as great as it is unreasonable . . . But I wonder sometimes if its madness doesn't hide more reason and more wisdom than you think. (*a pause*) Father, you have nothing to say?

ARENAS. I am listening . . .

VINCENT PINZÓN. I'd be happy to know your opinion.

ARENAS. I expected that question. But I don't wish to answer it . . .

VINCENT PINZÓN. You want to avoid the issue?

ARENAS. My son, I must watch over interests different from yours, and I don't feel qualified to take part in your debate. Besides . . .

MARTIN PINZÓN. (*interrupting him*) Quiet, friends. Here is Alonzo. *Alonzo appears at the door.*

Scene II

ALONZO. Gentlemen, the Admiral begs you to pardon his delay. The Governor of the island kept him longer than he'd expected. He'll be along in a moment.

MARTIN PINZÓN. He has seen the Governor?

ALONZO. He has just taken leave of him.

VINCENT PINZÓN. (*softly*) Taken leave . . .

ALONZO. Gentlemen, I have important news for you.

ARENAS. We can read it on your face.

19

ALONZO. I can't hide my joy, Father . . . We sail this morning.

MARTIN PINZÓN. You are sure?

ALONZO. The Admiral will tell you himself.

MARTIN PINZÓN. The men know it?

ALONZO. Not yet.

MARTIN PINZÓN. Let him go and tell them, too!

ALONZO. He will, Captain Pinzón, rest assured.

VINCENT PINZÓN. What time are we leaving, Alonzo?

ALONZO. As soon as this conference is over.

VINCENT PINZÓN. Well, half your wishes are thereby granted, brother. We are weighing anchor. It is true that it's to take a direction that's not exactly the one you wanted . . .

MARTIN PINZÓN. I may have a few words to say on the subject.

As he speaks, Columbus enters.

Scene III

COLUMBUS. (*softly*) I am listening, Captain Pinzón.

MARTIN PINZÓN. Admiral . . .

COLUMBUS. (*continuing softly*) You had something you wished to report to me.

MARTIN PINZÓN. Yes.

COLUMBUS. I said I was listening.

MARTIN PINZÓN. This expedition is suicide, and you should know it. Our ships are incapable of making three hundred leagues without leaking at every seam. And we have no idea whether the distance may not be two or three times that.

COLUMBUS. Whatever the distance, God willing, we will cover it.

MARTIN PINZÓN. And our return?

COLUMBUS. This is not the time to think of it.

MARTIN PINZÓN. Ask your crew if that's what they think.

COLUMBUS. Whom else should I consult?

MARTIN PINZÓN. It's too easy to ignore them. They're the ones who must follow you.

COLUMBUS. I'm not ignoring them. I have more confidence in them than I have in you. Is that all that you have to tell me?

MARTIN PINZÓN. I repeat . . .

COLUMBUS. Enough. I asked if you had anything else to tell me.

MARTIN PINZÓN. No.

COLUMBUS. Then I will speak. Is it you, Captain Pinzón, who broke your ship's rudder?

MARTIN PINZÓN. What do you mean?

COLUMBUS. You know perfectly well what I mean. I'm asking if you're the one who broke the *Pinta*'s rudder. The workmen who repaired it are absolutely sure that the rudderpost did not break of its own accord. Someone sawed it in two. And I ask you for the last time if that someone was you.

MARTIN PINZÓN. No.

COLUMBUS. It was one of your men then.

MARTIN PINZÓN. I can answer for them as for myself.

COLUMBUS. That's just what makes me suspect them! (*a pause*) It is fortunate for you that I lack the time to seek out the guilty party. This time I shall pass over the incident . . . But I warn you that in the future I shall hold you responsible for any mishap of this nature that should affect your ship. Have you understood?

MARTIN PINZÓN. Yes.

COLUMBUS. Naturally that goes for you, too, Vincent . . .

VINCENT PINZÓN. I accept my responsibility.

COLUMBUS. Now I shall speak to all of you. We shall sail in exactly one hour. Until then — but only until then — I am ready to answer your questions and to take your observations into consideration . . . I am even ready to land on the island those who lack the courage to face this expedition, or who refuse to submit to my authority. They can easily find a ship to take them back to Spain . . . Does anyone wish to avail himself of this opportunity? (*a pause*) Captain Pinzón?

MARTIN PINZÓN. I will not leave my ship.

COLUMBUS. Very well. I conclude that you are all ready to follow my orders. You will continue then in command of your ships. Alonzo will remain with me . . . As for you, Father . . .

ARENAS. (*interrupting him, softly*) I must remind you, Admiral, that I am responsible solely to His Eminence, the Cardinal of Spain.

21

COLUMBUS. I do not contest your spiritual authority. I was indeed going to tell you that you will exercise your ministry in complete freedom on these ships. But I must remind you that the material conduct of this expedition has been confided to me, and that, in this domain, I am in sole charge.

ARENAS. After God, whom I represent.

COLUMBUS. After God. (*Columbus turns and points to the map stretched out on the table*) Gentlemen, here is the map of the ocean . . . Here is Spain. Here are the islands that we are going to leave behind . . . There, somewhere, far to the west, lies India!

VINCENT PINZÓN. How far, Admiral?

COLUMBUS. I do not know.

VINCENT PINZÓN. You intend to sail at night?

COLUMBUS. We shall sail day and night for seven hundred leagues. Beyond that, we shall heave to between midnight and dawn. (*a pause*) Alonzo, what is the state of our provisions?

ALONZO. We have food and firewood for a year, Admiral. Drinking water for eight months.

COLUMBUS. With God's help, that should suffice. (*a pause*) Now, Gentlemen, we are going to separate, and you will go back to your ships. We shall soon be irrevocably at sea. Irrevocably! You must understand what that means! That means that I will not turn back without having reached my goal. God has designated us for one of the greatest missions He ever confided to any one of His creatures. We must work to be worthy of the blessing He has granted us. Neither fatigue nor fear nor disappointments nor suffering must stop us. Never for a second forget that the Cross of Christ stretches out its arms on our sails! (*a pause*) Now go! May God keep you! (*Darkness. Followed immediately by*)

THIRD TABLEAU

Same setting as for the First Tableau: the deck of the Santa Maria. *September 26, 1492, about six p.m. Dusk. The guitar plays the same theme as in the First Tableau. It gradually stops, to begin again at the end of the scene.*

CHORUS.

So now it is too late.

The time prophesied by the evil prophets has arrived.

We have heard the whipping of the mainsail, the grating of the anchor being raised . . .

And destiny, which placed us in God's hands, at the same time, was set in motion.

Now it is too late.

FIRST VOICE.

Too late for regret, too late for hope!

SECOND VOICE.

Too late for pardon!

CHORUS.

We are alone. Nothing but the ocean around us, the relentless ocean.

Nothing but that long wrinkle of foam from one end to the other of the horizon.

THIRD VOICE.

The wave slowly lifts us up, then falls back into this strange leaden twilight.

FOURTH VOICE.

It is six o'clock. A beautiful evening. One hundred twenty men suddenly fall silent and watch.

CHORUS.

Do not punish us, O Lord. If we have sinned, we have sinned unknowingly.

Sinned like each and everyone. Nothing serious and never very often!

FIRST VOICE.

Sometimes when distracted in church, sometimes when absent . . .

SECOND VOICE.

A few oaths . . .

THIRD VOICE.

A violent burst of anger from time to time . . .

FOURTH VOICE.

And when one wanted love, there was that wench who happened by . . .

CHORUS.

O Lord, our only sins have been anger and lust.

To forget our sleepless nights, our meager living and our misery,

To avenge ourselves on unjust fate, to defend ourselves from misfortune,

we had only that woman beside us and this great cry that came from our hearts!

O Lord, we have lived in sin, but we know now that we need only You . . .

Do not abandon us to the eternity of this solitude, to the seduction of this desert!

FIRST VOICE.

When we left, I held her against my heart . . .

In the corner of her eye she had a tear, one little tear that she let fall.

SECOND VOICE.

Six in the evening. One day more has gone by.

CHORUS.

While the strumming of the guitar resumes

This is the end of our desires,

our sins and our pleasures:

all that we have loved,

snowy winter, torrid summer,

the taste of an apple in the orchard,

all gone now in the great liquid injustice

in which our kisses melt.

The guitar grows louder.

Darkness. Followed immediately by

FOURTH TABLEAU

Columbus's cabin. Columbus and Alonzo together as the curtain rises.

COLUMBUS. No, Alonzo, I have confidence in no one. Through these long years I have learned to distrust them. Those I have caressed have so often tried to bite me that I have come to suspect all sincere gestures. I have never received so much as from those creatures from whom I expected nothing. What do they want of me this time?

ALONZO. They would like to discuss the situation with you.

COLUMBUS. Both of them?

ALONZO. Especially Martin Pinzón. He insists on it bitterly, almost insolently . . .

COLUMBUS. What reasons does he give?

ALONZO. Always the same, Admiral . . . The length of the expedition, the course to take, the impatience of his crew . . .

COLUMBUS. And his brother?

ALONZO. Vincent is more adaptable. He submits to your good guidance, and sends, with his compliments, some fresh fish that his men have caught.

COLUMBUS. Hm . . . I don't know which one I prefer . . .

ALONZO. What should I answer, Admiral?

COLUMBUS. Tell them I see no reason to advance the date of our council. I will see them within three days, as was agreed.

ALONZO. And the present Vincent sends you?

COLUMBUS. Send it back!

ALONZO. Wouldn't accepting it be the wiser move, Admiral?

COLUMBUS. No. If I thus fail to recognize real devotion, I shall excuse myself for it later. For the moment, I want to maintain the exact balance between the two brothers . . . Thank him and tell him that I wish to share the rations of my crew.

ALONZO. Good.

COLUMBUS. Have you nothing else to report? How are the men?

ALONZO. Until now better than I would have believed, Admiral . . .

COLUMBUS. No infractions of discipline?

25

ALONZO. None. Rather the appearance of resignation . . . But their state of mind changes like the wind. Today they are calm. Tomorrow, they may be raving mad . . .

COLUMBUS. They are children . . .

ALONZO. Some of them, all the same, must be watched.

COLUMBUS. Which ones?

ALONZO. Roldán and Ruiz, especially. Perez also. I know they are trying to stir up the others!

COLUMBUS. What are they thinking? What are they saying?

ALONZO. It has been impossible for me to find out, Admiral. They all take great pains to avoid me, for they suspect that I come to them representing you. I think there's only one man who can tell you about them.

COLUMBUS. Arenas? I thought of that . . . I asked him to stop in to see me.

ALONZO. He has all their confidence.

COLUMBUS. I can well believe it . . . The man who promises eternal life to those who fear death is always a powerful consoler. (*a pause*) Here he comes . . .

Arenas appears at the door.

Scene II

ARENAS. You sent for me, Admiral?

COLUMBUS. Yes, Father. I'm not taking too much of your time? You were probably busy.

ARENAS. Oh, a few confessions . . . Nothing out of the ordinary . . .

COLUMBUS. I realize that one hundred twenty men do not constitute a meager flock . . . (*a pause*) It's really about them that I wanted to speak to you. You know them well, do you not?

ARENAS. My position demands that I do, my son.

COLUMBUS. You are their friend . . .

ARENAS. I try at least to be their guide, as I try to be yours . . .

COLUMBUS. Father, let's stop speaking of me, shall we? For the moment, it is the crew that matters . . . The success of our venture rests above all on the help these men will give me. And I am aware that you know more about them than I do. When I draw near them, they fall silent. When I speak to them, they draw away.

ARENAS. What can I do for you?

COLUMBUS. I want to know what they are thinking, what they fear, what they're dreaming.

ARENAS. You want to know? (*He goes to the porthole and opens it. On the guitar is heard the theme that introduces the chorus*) Listen to them. That is what they think . . .

COLUMBUS. (*slamming the porthole shut*) Madness! . . .

ARENAS. That is all they have left, my son: their guitar, gambling, and, in their spare time, God . . . Look at them!

COLUMBUS. (*looking out through the porthole*) All at the stern, their faces turned toward the east.

ARENAS. As if, beyond seven hundred leagues of ocean, they could still see the coasts of Spain! (*a pause*) It is true that you can make out India from even farther . . .

COLUMBUS. They are throwing dice . . .

ARENAS. I'm sorry you can't hear their bets . . . They are wild. Those who long ago lost their pay now bet memories, summer sunlight . . . Alfonso Perez yesterday lost the shade of his vineyard. He laughed about it, for he is certain that the man who won it will never enjoy sitting under it! (*a pause*) I have watched men condemned to death play like that in the courtyard of the prison at Córdoba.

COLUMBUS. (*to Alonzo, after a pause*) Leave us a moment, Alonzo, will you? I'll send for you in a little while.

Alonzo leaves, while Arenas glances at the books scattered on Columbus's table.

Scene III

COLUMBUS. What would your answer be, Father, if I proposed an alliance with you?

ARENAS. I am listening . . .

27

COLUMBUS. United, your power and mine would be invincible. We could triumph together . . .

ARENAS. Over what? Every alliance is a bargain of sorts, my son. What do you offer me?

COLUMBUS. My name.

ARENAS. That is all?

COLUMBUS. Twenty years of struggle and suffering, the burden of my great plan, my life.

ARENAS. I fear that may be insufficient. Your power, as you point out, needs mine perhaps. Mine does not need yours. In what respect does your glory interest God?

COLUMBUS. I offer him an immense country lost in darkness, thousands of forests and rivers, millions of souls that He does not know.

ARENAS. This time it's perhaps too much, my son.

COLUMBUS. That is your answer?

ARENAS. I do not have your ambition. The few souls in danger that have been confided to me on these ships are enough for me, for the entire Kingdom of God is struggling within each one of them. I shall be sure not to have lost my life, if I succeed in saving just one!

COLUMBUS. You refuse me then.

ARENAS. I didn't say that . . . I wish only to temper your zeal. Its excess seems to me sinful.

COLUMBUS. All right.

ARENAS. The first commandment of any living creature is to know his limitations, my son. I was looking at your books just now. (*He takes them up and goes over their titles*) Esdras, Vegetius, Toscanelli . . . How many pages, and what oblivion! (*He drops the books angrily*) All this science is the image of our vanity . . .

COLUMBUS. Or of our love! We find in it what we bring to it, Father.

ARENAS. Have you the illusion of having learned in these books one thing, one single thing, that was worth knowing?

COLUMBUS. Yes.

ARENAS. I should be happy to know it, also.

COLUMBUS. (*pointing to one of the books*) Take this book.

ARENAS. (*disdainfully*) Seneca . . .

COLUMBUS. Open it. The page is marked.

ARENAS. (*reading*) *Venient annis saecula* . . .

COLUMBUS. (*interrupting him*) "A time will come in the long history of the world, when the sea will break its bonds . . . A part of the earth will open up, and a sailor, like the one who was Jason's guide, will discover a new world. Then Thule will not be the outermost land . . ."

ARENAS. So you also know Latin?

COLUMBUS. Alonzo translated this passage for me.

ARENAS. Alonzo?

COLUMBUS. When I met him, he was a student at Salamanca.

ARENAS. I didn't know that the University taught navigation.

COLUMBUS. It doesn't. He was preparing for the priesthood.

Arenas stares at him.

ARENAS. Is that your trap? You have turned him away from his vocation.

COLUMBUS. He came to me, knowing that on my ships he could also serve God.

ARENAS. You are not unaware, I suppose, what a great responsibility you bear?

COLUMBUS. I am so well aware of it, Father, that I counted on speaking to you of him. He's even one of the reasons that led me to ask to talk with you. (*a pause*) Given the state of mind of the crew, an accident might happen to me at any time. It must not ruin the success of this expedition. I intend to make Alonzo my successor.

ARENAS. To bind him all the more firmly . . .

COLUMBUS. To reward his fidelity and honor his merits.

ARENAS. Then what do you expect me to do? Approve of your decision?

COLUMBUS. Father, legally you have no power to do so. And morally . . .

ARENAS. (*interrupting him*) I perhaps do not have the taste to do so.

COLUMBUS. (*bowing*) I shall ask you then only a slight favor. To be the witness of my decision. If I were to disappear, there would undoubtedly be some disturbance on board. I trust that the word of a minister of God will carry in the quarrels between men . . .

ARENAS. Very well. I accept. Is that all?

COLUMBUS. That is all, Father. I am sorry that we did not understand each other better. I'd have liked you to become my friend.

ARENAS. I am no man's enemy, my son. But I confess that the state in which I find you causes me the greatest anxiety . . .

COLUMBUS. (*after a long pause, very wearily*) If you meet Alonzo, Father, will you send him to me?

Arenas leaves. For a short while Columbus remains alone on stage. He sinks down wearily and looks at the crucifix. Then Alonzo enters without making a sound.

Scene IV

ALONZO. Admiral, you need me?

COLUMBUS. Yes, Alonzo . . . On that table, you will find an envelope. Take it . . . (*Alonzo goes toward the table and takes the envelope*) It contains private orders which are meant for you . . . (*Alonzo starts to open the envelope*) No, do not open it. Only after my death.

ALONZO. Your death?

COLUMBUS. (*softly*) One must foresee every eventuality, Alonzo . . .

ALONZO. May I ask you one question, Admiral?

COLUMBUS. None, on this subject.

ALONZO. Very well. (*Alonzo, still gazing at Columbus, hides the envelope in his doublet. A pause*) You have not dictated your entry in the log, Admiral.

COLUMBUS. True. You may begin. (*Alonzo sits at the table, lights the lamp, and opens a large logbook. Columbus rises. During the remainder of the scene, he strides up and down, dictating*) Wednesday, September 26, fifty-fourth day of our journey. Sailed, during night and day, thirty-one leagues to the west. The sea is calm. Sighted many dorado and other fish. During the morning, however, the sky clouded over and a fine rain fell, obscuring the hor-

30

izon. Still no sign of land, except for some masses of green weed, drifting toward the east . . ."

Columbus has approached the porthole while dictating. He hesitates a moment, then opens it. The sad song of the guitar pours into the cabin. Columbus listens, lowering his head, and Alonzo, who has stopped writing, sits motionless.

CURTAIN

Act II

The deck of the Santa Maria. *September 29, 1492, eleven o'clock in the morning. Still the same theme on the guitar.*

A VOICE.

Fifty-seven days! Already fifty-seven days since we left Palos!

SECOND VOICE.

Fifty-seven days, fifty-seven nights!

CHORUS.

There is not a wave on the sea, not a breath of air in the sky . . .
It is warm and clear for Michaelmas.

THIRD VOICE.

Torrid August has given way to tepid September without our having seen the color of the water change . . .

FOURTH VOICE.

. . . nor the color of the sky.

FIRST VOICE.

Fifty-seven times the sun has plunged under our prow into the still, flat ocean . . .

SECOND VOICE.

. . . without any news from our families.

THIRD VOICE.

Fifty-seven days, fifty-seven nights!

CHORUS.

In Palos, at Michaelmas, the girls dance in the gardens of the Passetta!

FOURTH VOICE.

Under a cypress trembling with birds — that's where I met her. We
danced all day long . . .

CHORUS.

In Palos, at Michaelmas! . . .

FIRST VOICE.

We drink cool wine on our thresholds as we speak of the events of
the day.

SECOND VOICE.

Evening is as gentle as love . . .

THIRD VOICE.

In Palos, at Michaelmas . . .

CHORUS.

Is it then too much to ask that we be allowed that at least?

Those hours that were so precious to us, but we did not know it!

Lord, give us our poverty, our little hopes, our poor harvests!

Give us back the wretchedness which is our lot and with which we
feel at ease!

We don't need much: a little love, a little conversation, three po-
tatoes on the coals.

We do not need much: we are very ordinary people,

people without ambition, without great plans,

people made for ordinary things . . .

Lord, give us back our bare orchards, our sterile fields.

Even if the barn is empty, even if the child weeps in its mother's
arms,

give us back Your blessing in mourning and in dust,

O Lord, if it is Your will that we die, may Your will be done!

But if we cannot choose the place of our death and the form of
our final agony,

Lord,

before the final blow that we shall await upon our knees,

give us back, for a second,

the perfume of all Spain in a breath of wet wind!

Give us back, Lord, all the loveliness of the world,

the happiness of summer, the color of the sky

in the fragrance of a ripe pomegranate
split open
in Palos, at Michaelmas.
Darkness. Followed immediately by

SECOND TABLEAU

Columbus's cabin.

Scene I

MARTIN PINZÓN. This time, Alonzo, he will have to listen to us!

ALONZO. You will speak with him in a moment.

VINCENT PINZÓN. (*going toward a porthole*) Where is he?

ALONZO. In the map room, charting our course.

MARTIN PINZÓN. Our course, Alonzo? We've been motionless for two days.

ALONZO. I mean that he is measuring the distance we have already covered.

VINCENT PINZÓN. (*gazing out*) The sea is as calm as the river of Seville. You can see fish glide under the water . . .

MARTIN PINZÓN. Doesn't this persistent calm worry the Admiral?

ALONZO. He says that God will take care of that.

VINCENT PINZÓN. God has much to do . . .

MARTIN PINZÓN. And our men much too little!

ALONZO. Can you complain of them?

MARTIN PINZÓN. Just as much, I suppose, as you can complain of yours!

ALONZO. I see . . .

VINCENT PINZÓN. And you, Alonzo?

ALONZO. What do you want to know?

VINCENT PINZÓN. Your feeling about the situation.

ALONZO. I am not a part of the crew, Captain, and I exercise no command on this vessel. It is neither my position to submit nor to decide . . .

VINCENT PINZÓN. You are avoiding a direct reply! Everyone knows your influence in the Admiral's councils . . .

ALONZO. Possibly.

MARTIN PINZÓN. Answer us, Alonzo!

ALONZO. (*after a pause*) No, Captain Pinzón.

MARTIN PINZÓN. As you like. But pray God that your discretion armor you for the day when you will be held accountable.

ALONZO. Accountable to you?

MARTIN PINZÓN. Accountable perhaps to the lowest cabin boy on the lowest of our ships.

ALONZO. His crime would be less great than yours!

MARTIN PINZÓN. Less great also than your pride.

VINCENT PINZÓN. Quiet, both of you! You are mad, brother. Where does this anger lead you? The situation demands that we keep calm. (*a pause*) Alonzo, you have misjudged the meaning of our questions. I am not opposed to this expedition. On the contrary. My brother will tell you how much he and I differ on the subject . . . I believe, however, that the Admiral should be informed of the state of mind of the crew.

ALONZO. He is.

VINCENT PINZÓN. I don't think so. He may know what the situation is here on this ship . . . But he does not know what it is like on the *Pinta* or the *Niña* . . . Our men truly have difficulty controlling their impatience.

ALONZO. Do they think you can go from Spain to India as easily as from Palos to Cartagena?

VINCENT PINZÓN. What they think, Alonzo, we don't know. They are simple souls, as difficult for you to fathom as it is difficult for them to fathom you.

ALONZO. In any case, I can easily fathom your soul.

MARTIN PINZÓN. (*threateningly*) And what do you see in it?

ALONZO. (*looking him up and down*) Treason that lies between fear and shame.

Martin starts forward. His brother holds him back slightly.

VINCENT PINZÓN. Be careful, Alonzo! My brother is going to seize you by the throat! His honor is as ticklish as a woman's armpit . . .

ALONZO. I am ready to answer to you.

VINCENT PINZÓN. No need to; I don't feel offended. And had I been, I would pardon you.

ALONZO. I don't need your forbearance.

MARTIN PINZÓN. You prefer our anger?

ALONZO. I prefer nothing that comes from you!

VINCENT PINZÓN. Alonzo . . . Your devotion is a very natural feeling that astonishes no one. What astonishes me is the point to which you carry it.

ALONZO. What do you mean?

VINCENT PINZÓN. Why does one always have the impression that you are forcing yourself? As if you were trying to breathe at a height unsuited to you. Look at the Admiral . . . He is at ease in his greatness, like an eagle at the height of heaven! You make me think of a titmouse fluttering its ears . . .

ALONZO. Really?

VINCENT PINZÓN. Oh, I don't suspect you of any baseness . . . On the contrary. It takes a certain courage to live beyond one's means.

ALONZO. Allow me to indulge myself to that extent.

VINCENT PINZÓN. (*bowing*) Someone has said that gazing upon noble souls . . .

Enter Columbus on these words.

Scene II

COLUMBUS. . . . is the ecstasy of God.

VINCENT PINZÓN. Exactly.

MARTIN PINZÓN. We are happy to see you, Admiral.

COLUMBUS. I should be pleased to say as much, Captain Pinzón. But, in fact, I don't want councils held in my absence.

VINCENT PINZÓN. We were waiting for you . . .

COLUMBUS. If you wish to speak to me, I beg you to be brief.

MARTIN PINZÓN. Admiral, the situation does not call for long speeches. The day of our departure, you yourself estimated that this expedition would last one month. Fifty-seven days have elapsed, and no land is in sight. We would like to know your intentions.

COLUMBUS. And then?

MARTIN PINZÓN. You asked us to be brief.

COLUMBUS. My reply will therefore be even briefer than your question: our journey will continue.

MARTIN PINZÓN. For how long?

COLUMBUS. As long as it will take us to reach the coast of India.

VINCENT PINZÓN. If the ocean remains as it is, you will need patience, Admiral.

COLUMBUS. I have patience, much patience, Vincent. Patience is a virtue that the folly of men has taught me for a long time.

MARTIN PINZÓN. The men have nothing to do with this absence of wind. God alone . . .

COLUMBUS. God has blessed this voyage. He will soon breathe into our sails.

MARTIN PINZÓN. Or else raise a hurricane to crush us.

COLUMBUS. Those are the risks of the ocean. Are you sailors?

MARTIN PINZÓN. A sailor watches over the life of his crew and the safety of his vessel.

COLUMBUS. A sailor carries out the orders given to him.

MARTIN PINZÓN. Unless they come from a sick brain. Maritime law provides that the madness of the captain releases one from the duty to obey.

COLUMBUS. It provides also for the penalty imposed on mutineers. Captain Pinzón, your language is beginning to displease me.

MARTIN PINZÓN. I am sorry. I am one of those who believe that a ship is not guided by dreams.

COLUMBUS. You are going to find out that men can be led by force. I give you twenty seconds to formulate your apology . . . (*A pause. All are silent*) All right. You are relieved of your command. You are under arrest.

VINCENT PINZÓN. (*coming between them*) Admiral, if there is still time, I would like to offer you the apology demanded by my brother's rather foolish conduct.

MARTIN PINZÓN. Did I ask you? . . .

VINCENT PINZÓN. I am sure that he will not be opposed to it, and I dare hope that you will accept it . . .

Columbus reacts visibly.

VINCENT PINZÓN. For I have the feeling that I am doing you a service . . . By sparing Captain Pinzón a disgrace that he has perhaps merited, I am at the same time sparing you a mistake.

COLUMBUS. Be careful also, Vincent, lest your excessive shrewdness lead you to an even greater one!

VINCENT PINZÓN. I fear there is no greater error right now than the disunion of command. Think of the crew, Admiral! You don't know the men you command . . . Ask Alonzo! We were speaking of them just now. The sailors of Palos are easily upset, and today's idleness, linked with the anxiety of a voyage that is much too long, as well as the dangers that they sense in the future, makes them capable of every sort of folly.

COLUMBUS. What folly? I demand that you speak clearly.

VINCENT PINZÓN. I fear that our discord will be the pretext for a mutiny . . .

COLUMBUS. Which you would lead!

VINCENT PINZÓN. Of which I, like you, might be the victim . . . I feel I have, until now, faithfully carried out your orders.

COLUMBUS. I want facts, not feelings.

VINCENT PINZÓN. I surprised one of my men just now sawing the cable of the rudder right in two. I put him in irons, awaiting your decision.

COLUMBUS. And then?

VINCENT PINZÓN. Underhand agitation of the crew, groups forming, talk stopping when I approach, but talk in which I know you are being attacked . . .

COLUMBUS. All right. What do you propose?

VINCENT PINZÓN. In your place, Admiral, I would begin by having a few men hanged.

COLUMBUS. Hanged! . . . Are you serious, Yáñez Pinzón?

VINCENT PINZÓN. If you wish to continue this expedition, you will find that you will need guilty men!

COLUMBUS. We will need heroes, and we'll not make them with victims.

MARTIN PINZÓN. Nor with speeches . . .

COLUMBUS. You are still there, Captain Pinzón? My word, I was about to forget you . . . Go back to your ship, and stay there! Show him back, Alonzo . . . (*The two captains and Alonzo start to leave*) And you, Vincent, stay . . .

Martin Pinzón and Alonzo leave.

Scene III

COLUMBUS. Your brother is an insolent fellow, Yáñez Pinzón, and I wouldn't be astonished if he were rather stupid also. But he possesses at least a virtue which you lack: he is frank . . . It suddenly occurs to me that I still don't know your opinion on the continuation of this expedition.

VINCENT PINZÓN. It is difficult for me to answer, Admiral . . .

COLUMBUS. You refuse?

VINCENT PINZÓN. I did not say that. But you asked me to be frank . . . It's a lucky man who can see only one side of things.

COLUMBUS. There is but one truth, Yáñez Pinzón!

VINCENT PINZÓN. So you affirm, Admiral . . . Don't you see, I sometimes strengthen my heart against you with very reasonable thoughts. Then my softest voice speaks out, but it is a voice not lacking in weight: "Vincent Yáñez Pinzón," it whispers in my ear, "are you forgetting that you are not only the captain but also the owner of the *Niña*? Have you lost all good sense to risk your life and your fine ship in such a mad adventure? Return to Palos, where your friends await you, your wife, and your great house on Trinity Square." That's what that voice tells me, and to be more persuasive, it whispers memories . . . You are never troubled, Admiral, by your memories?

COLUMBUS. My memories . . . I remember especially the way the world dealt with me.

VINCENT PINZÓN. I'm speaking of little things: the taste of light wine drunk one evening on a terrace, while watching the mountains turn blue, the laugh of a woman in the deepening night, the gaze of a friend . . .

COLUMBUS. I have no friends, with the exception of Alonzo.

VINCENT PINZÓN. The color of a summer dawn on the Sanlúcar road, the hop of the first grasshopper in the dust . . . Ah, the memory of dust, on a ship . . .

COLUMBUS. Enough, Vincent! Whom do you hope to upset?

VINCENT PINZÓN. No one, Admiral. No one but myself . . .

COLUMBUS. Since you wish to speak of memories, I should like you to remember that other Yáñez Pinzón, who signed up to follow me all the way.

VINCENT PINZÓN. He exists also . . . You see, it isn't all so simple! (*a pause*) At night when the heat prevents me from sleeping, I venture out at times to the prow of the *Niña*. When the moon is hidden, it is a strangely solitary place. Some distance from the ship, one can't even see the ocean; it's as if it had been drunk by the night sky. And there is, in front of the *Niña*, only this great curtain of darkness, this whirlpool of darkness and stars in which it sinks slowly down like a blind bird . . . I like to stand there for a long time, my coat open on my chest. I breathe in that air mixed with salt which comes to me from the land that you seek, while the wind, in the rigging, makes above my head the sound of a sort of lyre. And then I find myself without hope and without thought, detached from the time that I have lived, careless of the future which will be shaped for me. Because, for the first time, I have the sensation of being inscribed in my exact place in the order of the things of this world . . . Then I hear my heart whisper softly to me that you are right, and that a ship may well be guided by dreams . . .

COLUMBUS. (*softly*) Vincent, I need your help.

VINCENT PINZÓN. I'd like to help you.

COLUMBUS. All you need do is have your ship follow mine.

VINCENT PINZÓN. Are you sure that my men will allow me to have it follow yours?

COLUMBUS. Still that same fear . . . You must learn that faith is a gift that is transmitted, Vincent.

VINCENT PINZÓN. Less readily than fear!

COLUMBUS. These are children who tomorrow will laugh at their tears . . .

VINCENT PINZÓN. But children who today may slit our throats. You asked me for facts just now? Here is one that I had forgotten . . . You noticed yesterday those long weeds floating on the water? On board the *Niña* the members of the crew amused themselves by fishing them up with long poles. They pulled them in on the ship, and for a long time caressed their faces with them, in a kind of intoxication. Then they decked their bodies with these wet garlands, and began to dance . . .

COLUMBUS. Like children . . .

VINCENT PINZÓN. Like men in love. They love the earth. It was the earth's hair they were caressing.

COLUMBUS. I also love the earth, Vincent. I shall give it to them.

VINCENT PINZÓN. When?

COLUMBUS. I do not measure time. I told you that I was patient . . . I waited twenty years to undertake what your brother calls a mad scheme, and what I call God's design. I waited twenty years, and God waited twenty thousand years, before allowing me to come and revive the plan that lay dormant in His mind. What difference can a few weeks more make to God and me?

VINCENT PINZÓN. Does not that show excessive scorn for the creatures who accompany you?

COLUMBUS. On the contrary, it does them great honor to unfold to them a mission within the designs of Providence. (*a pause*) Vincent, I am transporting across the ocean a cargo of one hundred twenty worried men on whose shoulders rest the hope of Spain and the benediction of God! Whatever happens, I shall lead them to the port that has been indicated to me . . .

A great noise is heard on deck, a noise that resembles the flapping

41

of sails that are swelling with wind. The ship trembles all over.
Alonzo appears at the door.

ALONZO. Admiral, the wind is rising!

COLUMBUS. Do you hear, Vincent? Return to the *Niña*. Tonight, go
out on deck and look at the sky . . .
Darkness followed immediately by

THIRD TABLEAU

The deck of the Santa Maria, *the night of October 4, 1492. Same
setting. Columbus's lamp shines behind the porthole in his cabin. Still
the same theme on the guitar.*

FIRST VOICE.
Another night, says the Lord.
Another night for man . . .
I have covered the earth with a cloak, and have called it night.

SECOND VOICE.
A night to love, a night to sleep.

THIRD VOICE.
A night to weep, a night to die.

FOURTH VOICE.
A night filled with birds . . .

SECOND VOICE.
. . . a night filled with flowers.

FIFTH VOICE.
. . . a night filled with tears . . .

THIRD VOICE.
. . . a night filled with fear.

FIRST VOICE.
This is my most beautiful garden, says the Lord.
A pause.

CHORUS.
Three o'clock in the morning . . .

SECOND VOICE.

There is not a star in the sky, not a light on the water.

THIRD VOICE.

High up the lookout in the crow's nest, who has been watching since midnight, weary of having seen nothing, has finally fallen asleep.

CHORUS.

We are alone, watching the immensity of the world,

alone

with the lamp of Columbus.

Nothing but our poor lantern, whose flame flickers, whose wick turns to carbon,

and the proud lamp of Columbus.

All the distress of the world and all its ambition,

all the simplicity of the world and all its complication,

for a moment meet in a little light on the edge of this sad

    deck . . .

All the following responses come quickly and violently, one on top of the other.

FOURTH VOICE.

O lamp of pride . . .

FIFTH VOICE.

Light of arrogance and aberration . . .

FIRST VOICE.

Go out.

SECOND VOICE.

Disappear.

THIRD VOICE.

Return to the endless night in which you have imprisoned us.

FOURTH VOICE.

Too long have we been patient.

FIFTH VOICE.

Now we will be patient no longer.

FIRST VOICE.

We reject this delirium that you call courage . . .

SECOND VOICE.

  . . . this madness that you call reason.

CHORUS.

We also love God . . .

And we are wedded to the earth He has made for us, more faithfully than you.

We bear that earth in our hearts, and on it, slowly, our hands have worn themselves out.

We love it in the darkness of every night, in the light of every morning!

We love it in the grain and in the millstone, in the snow and in the wheat, in the spirit and in the bread.

But for us Europe is quite beautiful enough and Spain is sufficient.

We want no more of this profit that you offer us; we refuse this effort that you demand of us!

Let us go back, let us return to Palos, let us go back together.

May the wheel turn, may the sun at last rise before us.

There is still time, if you wish. We can still live, we can still be happy!

Three men rush toward Columbus's cabin.

FOURTH TABLEAU

Scene I

Columbus's cabin. The Admiral is seated in front of his table. The door has been thrust open violently, and three men rush into the room. They stop suddenly on seeing the Admiral . . . The door has remained open behind them, and, during the long silence that follows, one can hear distinctly the sound of the ocean, and, in gusts, the distant sound of a guitar. Columbus rises slowly.

COLUMBUS. (*softly*) Close the door, Pedro! (*Pedro Niño hesitates, then obeys. Columbus slowly approaches the group which is still motionless. He sees an ax in the hands of Bartholomew Roldán.*)

44

Do you chop wood in the middle of the night, Bartholomew? (*a pause*) Give me that ax. You might cut yourself . . .
He takes the ax and hurls it into a chest, without a word of protest from anyone.

PEDRO NIÑO. Excuse us, Admiral! We can't stand it any longer . . .

COLUMBUS. There are only three of you?

BARTHOLOMEW ROLDÁN. The others sent us to you.

COLUMBUS. Which others? All of them?

BARTHOLOMEW ROLDÁN. All, except one or two.

COLUMBUS. One or two . . . There are at least one or two men on board this ship who keep their word and have confidence in mine. That is more than I had hoped for.

PEDRO NIÑO. I told you; we can't go on . . .

BARTHOLOMEW ROLDÁN. (*almost at the same time*) Death is upon us.

COLUMBUS. And in order not to face death, you wanted to kill me?

BARTHOLOMEW ROLDÁN. God is my witness, Admiral!

COLUMBUS. (*interrupting him*) God does not much like traitors, Bartholomew.

SANCHO RUIZ. You think he likes madmen.

COLUMBUS. I was wondering when you would speak up, Sancho . . . Come here!

SANCHO RUIZ. (*approaching*) You will not frighten me!

COLUMBUS. I hope not . . . A sailor like you fears nothing except the sea . . . Did you tell your friends, Sancho, what your situation was before you signed on this vessel?

PEDRO NIÑO. He told us he was on another ship.

COLUMBUS. He was not lying . . . He was indeed a galley slave on another of His Majesty's ships. And for what crime? For participating in a mutiny! . . .

SANCHO RUIZ. Yes, we threw overboard a man of far greater value than you!

COLUMBUS. I obtained his parole. Now I have the right to have him hanged.

SANCHO RUIZ. If you are able.

COLUMBUS. That would not be difficult. I am sure that your friends

45

here would be willing to help me in that task. For they are honest sailors . . . but are just a little upset. Right, Pedro?

PEDRO NIÑO. We cannot continue like this, Admiral. We want to go home.

COLUMBUS. I promise you that you will go home.

PEDRO NIÑO. At once?

COLUMBUS. Soon . . . As soon as we have finished our job.

BARTHOLOMEW ROLDÁN. No, Admiral, it's useless. We have waited long enough, we have hoped long enough. We no longer have faith in your promises. We want to go back to Spain immediately.

COLUMBUS. Bartholomew, you distress me . . . When you used to fish off San Fernando, would you have returned to port with your hold empty and your nets without fish? And you, Pedro, if your thirty feet of vineyard had not borne fruit through your own fault, would you have dared look at your wife's face the night of the harvest?

SANCHO RUIZ. Don't listen to him.

COLUMBUS. On the contrary, do listen to me! For if you are deaf to the language of grandeur, I shall use the language of honesty and good sense. Let me first ask you a few questions . . . Pedro, have we lost a single man since our departure?

PEDRO NIÑO. No, Admiral.

COLUMBUS. Have we had a single day of bad weather? Have we encountered the least peril?

BARTHOLOMEW ROLDÁN. You do not understand me, Admiral . . . What disturbs us is the future. We have been traveling for sixty-two days on an unknown ocean, and always straight to the west. No navigator has ever attempted that . . .

COLUMBUS. It will indeed be my glory to have done it.

BARTHOLOMEW ROLDÁN. And the price of your glory will be our death . . .

COLUMBUS. There is no question of dying, but rather of carrying out a mission which we have accepted. If we were to turn around, I should be called the next day before the Queen. And what would I tell her? "Your Majesty, we sailed more than eight hundred leagues to the west, we encountered only compliant winds on our

46

way, we weathered no gale, nor experienced the slightest damage . . . But we come back to you, without having put ashore, with ships intact and food for a year, because we were afraid!" That is what you would send me to tell her?

SANCHO RUIZ. Don't listen to him. I tell you that if you listen to him, you are lost!

COLUMBUS. (*opening a porthole violently*) Off there, in the middle of the night, perhaps just a few leagues from the prows of our ships, an immense country awaits us, a land covered with idols and golden temples, to which it is our duty to bring the word of God! You have like me had the honor of being chosen among the men of all times and all nations to carry out this adventure . . . And you would like to give it up when there is nothing threatening you. I tell you now loud and clear: as long as I am alive, that shall not happen!

SANCHO RUIZ. (*throwing himself on Columbus*) And that is why I am going to kill you.

The two men grapple. Columbus seizes Sancho's hand, which holds a dagger. Pedro starts to move forward, but Bartholomew holds him back. Suddenly a great noise is heard on deck. Shouts. A rifle shot. The two men draw apart. Immediately afterward, Alonzo appears, holding in his hands a dead white bird.

Scene II

ALONZO. Admiral, a bird. The crew has just caught a bird. A messenger from the land of India. (*a pause*) What is the matter?

COLUMBUS. Nothing . . .

ALONZO. You are trembling . . .

COLUMBUS. It is nothing . . . The folly and baseness of the world tend sometimes to come back to me . . . Come close, all of you, and delight with me that God has sent us this sign of His approval! Just at this time, too . . . Right, Sancho?

SANCHO RUIZ. Your messenger is dead, Admiral. It will not announce anything to anyone . . .

COLUMBUS. It seems to be a kind of gull . . . What do you think of it, Alonzo?

ALONZO. I doubt that that bird can travel farther than twenty leagues from shore, Admiral.

COLUMBUS. Can we be that close?

ALONZO. Look. It still has sand between its feet . . .

SANCHO RUIZ. A dead bird . . . That's all we know of India!

COLUMBUS. Except I shall see in his hands the print of the nails, and thrust my hand into his side . . . Finish the quotation, Pedro.

PEDRO NIÑO. . . . I will not believe that he has risen from the dead.

COLUMBUS. Is it not a great wonder that God has sent us this bird at the very moment when you doubted Him and me?

PEDRO NIÑO. Yes, my lord.

COLUMBUS. (*wearily*) Good . . . Leave now . . . All of you . . . I will forgive you one more time.

They all leave. Darkness. Followed immediately by

FIFTH TABLEAU

The deck of the Santa Maria. *October 7, 1492, at ten o'clock in the morning. Same theme on the guitar.*

CHORUS.

So. No one has heard us . . .

We have spoken for nothing. We have cried out in the desert.

There is no salvation for us.

We have been at sea for two months: summer, they tell us, is over . . .

But what means have we of telling the seasons?

What means other than that pitiless sun that turns in the sky like a judge on his chair?

October on the water is like September, and summer, like autumn.

48

Yesterday is like today . . .
FIRST VOICE.
Still the wind rising, still the ocean breathing slowly.
SECOND VOICE.
The hopes of daylight . . .
THIRD VOICE.
. . . the terrors of night.
FOURTH VOICE.
Land glimpsed for a moment and then sinking into the fog . . .
FIRST VOICE.
And memory . . .
SECOND VOICE.
. . . and malice.
CHORUS.
We have been dispossessed of everything, we have been separated
from our hearts!
Sixty-five days in dereliction and fear,
since we weighed anchor alongside the quay on that pink and gray
morning . . .
Sixty-five days to learn to love life,
to weigh love with the weight of a breast, the price of a bird com-
ing to rest,
What was left us was not much, but we could live on it.
Sixty-five days to learn that yesterday we were men and that to-
morrow we shall be no more.
Certainly we have not always been happy . . .
But we were in our place where God had put us.
It was the order of the world and the course of things, and our
fathers had lived like this,
without great hope of a better world, without great desire to see it
change.
Richer even so than many who are rich, in spite of war and danger, in spite of winter famine and uncertain harvests.
Rich with a bit of light wind, an hour of shade at the fountain,
and evening peace in the orange grove . . .

THIRD VOICE.

Sixty-five days. Sixty-five days to interrogate heaven and to wring our hands.

FOURTH VOICE.

So much time to learn that the stars are everywhere the same, and that the ocean is endless.

FIRST VOICE.

Is that what you promised us, Columbus? Where are the treasures of Golconda?

CHORUS.

So many days to know that we are alone in the world . . .

For we have confessed, and we have not been absolved.

God has veiled his face, and He has turned away from us.

SIXTH TABLEAU

Columbus's cabin.

Scene I

ARENAS. My son, evil tongues are accustomed to affirming that the Church is slow to act . . . Regretfully I am going to prove them right. Do you know what I want to talk to you about?

COLUMBUS. I can guess . . .

ARENAS. My spiritual duties took me yesterday on the *Pinta.* I saw Martin Pinzón . . . You know he is very much against you.

COLUMBUS. I worry little about his feelings, Father.

ARENAS. You may be wrong . . . He reproaches you for many things . . .

COLUMBUS. For example?

ARENAS. I'll choose the least absurd. He says that you falsify the distance covered, so that the total you end up with is each day several leagues below that of the *Niña* or the *Pinta.*

COLUMBUS. He said that?

ARENAS. He states it categorically.

COLUMBUS. And why would I do that?

ARENAS. According to him, you would thus try to calm the apprehensions of the crew, by allowing a distance to show up that is really less than we have actually covered. But . . .

COLUMBUS. But?

ARENAS. But I should myself assign you a more subtle maneuver, one more in keeping with what I know of your character: hiding from everyone the exact location of the land that you would discover so that you alone may remain master of a secret . . .

COLUMBUS. Which is to be revealed only to Their Majesties.

ARENAS. So you recognize the fact?

COLUMBUS. Did I say so?

ARENAS. No, you did not say so. (*a pause*) However that may be, Martin Pinzón let me clearly understand that he is ready to abandon you.

COLUMBUS. That is too bad. But at this point of the voyage, two ships will be all I need.

ARENAS. Unless the contagion spreads to the crews of the others . . .

COLUMBUS. You may be sure that I will watch out that it does not.

ARENAS. The state of mind of these men deserves an attention . . .

COLUMBUS. That I do not cease to give, Father! Furthermore, I don't quite see your role in all this!

ARENAS. You don't quite see? You astonish me . . . I grant you that I don't need to concern myself with your little differences. Let Martin Pinzón take care of the safety of his ship, and let his men take care of their miserable lives, and you, of your success, I let you settle all that! . . . But there are other attentions which are mine alone, and which I owe to each of you. Because you are, for me, exactly the same as the others, and the Great Admiral of Spain differs no more from the deck hand who serves on the smallest of his ships than one shaft of grain from another in the fields harvested by the Lord. All souls are equally precious to God, my son. I should like you to think of that sometimes.

COLUMBUS. I think of it often, Father. I have the feeling that our enterprise does him honor through all the souls engaged in it.

ARENAS. That's exactly what I'm not sure about! . . . I fear on the contrary that the hearts burdened with a fear which is not that of Judgment may compromise their salvation, just as wheat wet by rain makes for a bread which tastes of water . . . As for you, my son, this voyage keeps you in a state of excitement and confusion which is certainly not good.

COLUMBUS. There is not one of my acts, Father, which is not dedicated to the glory of God!

ARENAS. Not one of your acts? . . . When I consider the abyss that is in my soul, your assurance terrifies me.

COLUMBUS. (*after a long pause*) I beg your pardon, Father. I was carried away by the intensity of my feeling.

ARENAS. Think of the immense responsibility that rests on your shoulders, my son! On these three ships, one hundred twenty men depend on you. Everything in them depends on you! Not only their lives — which I hold, like mine, to be of little consequence — but the very conditions under which their eternal lives are played out. If one of them were to perish through your fault in a state of mortal sin, would you consent to appear before God to answer to Him for it?

COLUMBUS. (*in the same tone of voice*) What do you advise me to do?

ARENAS. My son, the decision is not for me to take.

COLUMBUS. (*continuing, in the same tone of voice*) No . . . no, it is impossible . . . God cannot wish it!

ARENAS. (*gently*) You make yourself the interpreter of His intentions?

COLUMBUS. I try to understand them. And I am certain that He approves of me. He has given me a thousand proofs of it, a thousand signs, during the twenty years since He gave me this plan. And He communicated to me this power that has convinced the Queen and even the Cardinal of Spain . . . Father, will you deny the competence of Don Pedro González de Mendoza?

ARENAS. The approval that the Cardinal gave you — with much reticence, you will agree — does not cover the exceptional circumstances we are going through.

52

COLUMBUS. It covers the whole of an expedition which is not finished, and which I cannot renounce just because of some scruples.

ARENAS. Scruples? We have not understood each other, my son . . . And I see now that they were right to warn me against you.

COLUMBUS. How much I prefer your present tone, Father! How much good you do me! So you were warned against me?

ARENAS. What every single one of your sailors declares, and what I still refused to believe, is then quite true.

COLUMBUS. What are they saying?

ARENAS. They say that you believe yourself elected for the accomplishment of a divine mission. They say that you interpret the holy scriptures to make them serve the justification of your thesis.

COLUMBUS. Is that all?

ARENAS. They say that you invoke the intervention of miracles for support. And they cite at least two circumstances in which you have publicly thanked the Lord for this special protection . . . Several days ago, a bird delivered you from the fury of the crew. Somewhat earlier, it was the miraculous rising of the wind, after three days of calm, that you pointed to as proof of the favor that God granted you.

COLUMBUS. And what else?

ARENAS. On that last occasion, you said: "No one has experienced a similar miracle since the time Moses delivered Israel from its captivity." Is that correct?

COLUMBUS. I have nothing to account to you for.

ARENAS. Nothing?

COLUMBUS. Father, I am tired of your speeches and of your person. Have you some other communication to make to me?

ARENAS. I certainly have. I told you that I had come as a friend. You have refused the help I offered you. That is your right . . . But it is the priest who addresses you, and you are going to listen to him. It has been more than ten days, my son, since I heard your confession . . . I think this would be a good opportunity to ease your conscience of its sins.

COLUMBUS. I don't believe I have committed any since then, Father.

ARENAS. Just the thought of being exempt from them is already a sin, my son . . . Some humbler than you have been lost through pride.

COLUMBUS. I doubt that I possess the evenness of temper needed to speak to you, just as I doubt that you possess that needed to listen to me.

ARENAS. Now you cast doubt on my office.

COLUMBUS. I suspect the man you are of at times forgetting the habit he wears, of forgetting that he comes in the name of an order . . .

ARENAS. (*interrupting him brusquely*) I come in the name of Almighty God to order you to kneel here and now . . .

COLUMBUS. Very well. (*He kneels*)

ARENAS. May the Lord be in your heart and on your lips, so that you may confess all your sins . . . In the name of the Father and the Son and the Holy Ghost, Amen . . . I am listening, my son.

COLUMBUS. Father, I confess that I believe in God. I confess that I want His name glorified, and want His will to be done. I confess that I wish to see His kingdom grow over all the earth, to bring Christ to those people who are in ignorance and sin. I confess that I wish to fulfill the word of the Prophets, that I believe one must perpetuate the Holy spirit and extend it . . .

ARENAS. Enough.

COLUMBUS. (*rising*) I confess that I must carry out the commandment given by Isaiah: "Prepare ye the way of the Lord, make straight in the desert a highway for our God."

ARENAS. Enough!

COLUMBUS. (*standing up, his arms outstretched*) "Sing unto the Lord a new song, and praise from the end of the earth, ye that go down to the sea, and all that is therein; the isles, and the inhabitants thereof. For I the Lord thy God will hold thy right hand, saying unto thee, Fear not; I will help thee. Fear not, thou worm Jacob, and ye men of Israel! When thou passest through the waters, I will be with thee . . ."

ARENAS. (*striking the table violently*) Enough, I tell you. They will hear of your blasphemy. They will hear of your having held up to ridicule the sacrament of penitence. All your words will be reported!

COLUMBUS. I do not doubt your accuracy.

ARENAS. Do not above all doubt that you will be tried for your sacrilege! . . . And now I have exhausted my patience. I order you to relinquish your command and hand it over to Alonzo Quintanilla. He will take charge of returning these ships to Spain.

COLUMBUS. Father, for the last time, I tell you that this expedition will be carried to its conclusion!

ARENAS. It no longer has the approval of ecclesiastical authority.

COLUMBUS. I told you that it had the approval of God, and that is all I need.

ARENAS. All that remained for you to be was a rebel!

COLUMBUS. Father, all that remains for me to be is a martyr . . . I shall be perhaps through your good offices. But if God crowns my undertaking, it will cause such a stir throughout the world, and such thanks will be raised to Heaven, that your apologies and your pleas will echo less than the words of a deaf mute. This total risk that I still hesitated to take I now take thanks to you. And I thank you for giving me the courage to be finally, irrevocably, the man I am! (*He runs toward the door*) Alonzo! Alonzo! . . .

A pause. Alonzo appears.

Scene II

ALONZO. Admiral . . .

COLUMBUS. Alonzo, I have new orders to transmit to the three ships. They revoke all preceding orders. The death penalty will be administered at once to anyone who fails to obey them, whatever his rank, his function or his title . . . Will you take them down? (*Alonzo goes to the table, sits down, takes up a pen*) "Gatherings of more than four men, except for the requirements of duty, are forbidden. Access to the stern of the ship is forbidden to anyone not required there by the necessities of navigation. Gambling of any kind is henceforward forbidden on board. All guitars are to be confiscated. All conversations concerning Spain, the fatherland, love, and any events whatever that took place before our departure, are forbidden. The Salve Regina will be sung every evening by the entire crew . . . Crew members must be convinced that they are not taking part in an ordinary expedition, but in an undertaking that requires all their strength and the best of their souls, because it is just, conducted with pure intention, and in the service of God!" . . . That is all . . .

ALONZO. Admiral, you will not . . .

COLUMBUS. That is all, Alonzo! (*Alonzo bows without answering, and leaves. Arenas has not moved*) Father, our conversation is ended. You have done your duty. Allow me to do mine! . . .

CURTAIN

Act III

The deck of the Santa Maria, *October 11, 1492, the night of the discovery, at ten o'clock in the evening. No guitar. Three or four men, lying down or seated, in silence. One among them stands and speaks.*

A VOICE.

So we've reached the eleventh of October. It is ten P.M. The three ships did not move during the night; a great silence descended on them, and on all the ocean.

The two Pinzón brothers came on board the *Santa Maria.* They went directly to Columbus's cabin, where the reverend Father joined them. But the Admiral locked himself in the chart room and will not answer any call.

The crew also grew silent. Their guitars and their dice were taken away from them. And here they are around me, as on other nights, wrapped up in their jackets, seated or lying down, their eyes glazed. They have been forbidden to assemble, to speak to each other, to dream . . . But this regulation comes too late and is pointless. For these men have nothing more to say to each other, and they have even ceased waiting.

There are only these two left speaking as they stand slightly to one side . . . One is a convict saved from the gallows, and the other a Jew driven from Spain. By bringing together all that they have never had, they manage, even here, to lead a passable existence.

But the others, those who still have something to lose, have reached the point at which what is intolerable is not noticed any longer.

In short, a night like the preceding nights . . .

Total darkness, followed immediately by

SECOND TABLEAU

Columbus's cabin.

Scene I

ARENAS. Gentlemen, this state of things cannot last. I count on your support to put an end to it.

VINCENT PINZÓN. Father, you will understand our astonishment . . . The day of our departure, we consulted you, and you refused to answer us.

ARENAS. The situation then was different . . .The habit I wear, and the little taste that I feel for this type of business, forced me to remain outside your discussion! But since then . . .

VINCENT PINZÓN. (*softly*) I suppose that the Admiral has refused to take your advice?

ARENAS. He listens only to his pride! Still that would only concern his confessor, if what is at stake in this instance was not far beyond both his person and ours. That is why, if he agrees to see us — which I doubt — I should like for us to settle on a common approach. What is your feeling?

MARTIN PINZÓN. For me it is no longer a feeling, Father, but a decision. In a few hours we shall reach our seventy-third day of navigation. The expedition for me stops there. Tomorrow if no land has been sighted, the *Pinta* will sail back to Spain.

ARENAS. That seems to me an unwise decision, my son.

MARTIN PINZÓN. I don't see how any other is possible.

ARENAS. Think about it . . . Once you detach yourself from the

58

other ships, you become a mutineer, whatever happens . . . If the Admiral returns to Spain, he will see that you are hanged. And if he does not come back, you will have difficulty explaining why you are the sole survivor. No, believe me, it is your duty, and in your interest, not to abandon the common fate . . .

MARTIN PINZÓN. The Admiral will never consent to return, Father.

ARENAS. Then he must be made to consent to it.

MARTIN PINZÓN. We have tried.

ARENAS. The way you did was not good.

VINCENT PINZÓN. (*softly*) And what do you suggest?

ARENAS. It is not my role to suggest, my son. And still less to act . . . I am consulting you simply to obtain your opinion.

VINCENT PINZÓN. Once more, Father, yours at the moment would be infinitely precious to us.

ARENAS. Really? (*a pause*) Didn't they tell me that you had at one time the intention of seizing the Admiral, if you did not succeed in convincing him?

MARTIN PINZÓN. That idea did in fact cross our minds.

ARENAS. And you gave it up?

VINCENT PINZÓN. Father, a mutiny is a very serious act . . .

ARENAS. It's all a matter of terminology. Do they call a revolt against unjust power a mutiny? I think not. This revolt is the exercise of a right, and even a duty . . . Do you possess absolute proof that the Admiral has knowingly put his ships in danger, that he lacks the necessary competence to guide them, that he cuts down on the calculation of the distance covered with the aim of leading you into error? Do you or do you not possess these proofs?

MARTIN PINZÓN. I do.

ARENAS. Well then, secular courts will approve all the measures that you may take to assure the safety of your vessels. As for ecclesiastical authority, I shall deal with that . . .

MARTIN PINZÓN. If you give us your approval, Father . . .

ARENAS. You misunderstand me . . . I do not have the power to approve of things that do not concern me. The conduct of these ships is in your domain.

VINCENT PINZÓN. It's a matter of terminology, Father!

ARENAS. (*softly*) You are an insolent fellow, Yáñez Pinzón . . .

MARTIN PINZÓN. Am I to understand that your decisions make the meeting that we had in mind useless?

ARENAS. The Admiral will not receive you.

MARTIN PINZÓN. In that case, how shall we approach him?

ARENAS. Tonight . . . Take a few men . . .

MARTIN PINZÓN. And Alonzo?

ARENAS. I'll take care of Alonzo.

MARTIN PINZÓN. Good. Come, brother.

ARENAS. Why this suspicious haste, Captain Pinzón? Wait until you are rejected by the Admiral . . . If you allow me, I shall go find out his decision . . .

He leaves.

Scene II

VINCENT PINZÓN. He is right, brother. A little patience will add weight to your grievances . . . Not to mention that it will also allow you to remain a few minutes more in a world in which you are still a man, before entering another in which you will be nothing but a rascal!

MARTIN PINZÓN. What do you mean?

VINCENT PINZÓN. Didn't you hear what I said?

MARTIN PINZÓN. What's the matter with you?

VINCENT PINZÓN. Don't you find it admirable, brother, that the greatest undertakings of men hinge on so little? Here is an expedition that a single being has dreamed of for twenty years, that he has spent months preparing, weeks accomplishing, and which, on the eve of a possible discovery that would be perhaps the most illustrious in history, risks being broken off thanks to the five-minute discussion of a fanatic, a scatterbrain, and a dilettante! You will notice that I count myself with you . . .

MARTIN PINZÓN. What does this language mean, Vincent? If you have come this far with me . . .

VINCENT PINZÓN. It was to discuss the matter with the Admiral, not to betray him!

60

MARTIN PINZÓN. And what did you intend to ask him?

VINCENT PINZÓN. To reexamine the situation . . . But if he were to enter this cabin now, I would no longer ask that of him. Listening to you just now, I decided to follow him all the way. This morning you had succeeded in making me hesitate. I will hesitate no longer.

MARTIN PINZÓN. The wind from Spain has lost its fragrance?

VINCENT PINZÓN. It is I who have lost my regrets . . .

MARTIN PINZÓN. A strange conversion . . .

VINCENT PINZÓN. Isn't it?

MARTIN PINZÓN. So you want to discover India?

VINCENT PINZÓN. Why not?

MARTIN PINZÓN. Has it occurred to you that it perhaps does not exist on this side of the world? And that the Admiral . . .

VINCENT PINZÓN. What does it matter, brother, if he has sailed for the wrong place, if he has sailed for a good reason.

MARTIN PINZÓN. You have reached that point?

VINCENT PINZÓN. I have had time to think of many things as I listened to you . . . Particularly of this . . . There comes a moment in life when a man notices that he is growing old, and that he is growing old in vain. What he has possessed slips from his hands. What he has not possessed he will no longer be able to obtain. All that he loved has perished before him, or — what is worse — he has ceased to love it . . . And he finds himself alone, face to face with death, with the deeds that he has done, and his memories, like those fruits dried on the tree, whose taste, turned bitter, repulses even the birds. Being on that downward path, I admit that it would not displease me to die in a great action that would live on in the memory of mankind.

MARTIN PINZÓN. You certainly could not imagine a finer occasion.

VINCENT PINZÓN. And you, Captain Pinzón, do you think that after this adventure it will still be possible for you to board your little boat, and go from Palos to Moguer, and from Moguer to Palos, selling fish? I doubt it. You will keep within you, like a feeling of remorse, the nostalgia for a certain allegiance that you failed to keep.

MARTIN PINZÓN. I think you are mad, brother.

VINCENT PINZÓN. Perhaps . . . If madness is having lost the taste of what I am for the love of what is beyond me, then I am mad! But how marvellous that madness is!

MARTIN PINZÓN. You have allowed yourself to be seduced like a woman!

VINCENT PINZÓN. (*suddenly weary*) You do not understand . . .

MARTIN PINZÓN. I understand that we shall have to go ahead without you.

VINCENT PINZÓN. Go ahead, then! . . . I must point out to you, however, that the Admiral will be warned of your attempt.

MARTIN PINZÓN. You would dare betray us?

VINCENT PINZÓN. That is a word that I, in your place, brother, would not utter.

MARTIN PINZÓN. Words have little importance. Answer my question!

VINCENT PINZÓN. I have answered it . . . If a boat leaves your ship tonight, it will be sunk with all its occupants whoever they may be . . .

MARTIN PINZÓN. At two o'clock this morning a boat will be launched . . .

He goes toward the door.

VINCENT PINZÓN. Martin Alonzo! (*Pinzón stops. Vincent approaches him*) I beg you to be patient for a few days longer . . .

MARTIN PINZÓN. That is impossible! Do not insist . . . (*He turns his back on his brother, and starts to leave just as Arenas and Alonzo appear at the door. He draws back to let them pass*) Excuse me . . .

He leaves.

Scene III

ARENAS. Your brother seems in a great hurry, Vincent . . . What is happening?

VINCENT PINZÓN. Captain Pinzón asks that he be excused. He has been called back to his ship by important duties . . .

ARENAS. Really? (*a pause*) Alonzo, you had, I believe, a communication to make to these gentlemen?

ALONZO. The Admiral will not be able to receive you, Captain Pinzón. He regrets . . .

VINCENT PINZÓN. Did he say that he regretted?

ALONZO. Not exactly.

VINCENT PINZÓN. Then tell us what he said!

ALONZO. He wants you and your brother to refrain henceforth from coming on board this ship except in a case of absolute urgency. He believes that too frequent visits can only cause the crew undue anxiety.

VINCENT PINZÓN. And if a case of absolute urgency, as you say, brought me here?

ALONZO. You would have to present it to me first.

VINCENT PINZÓN. I see . . .

ARENAS. It seems to me that the Admiral takes care suddenly to keep very much to himself.

ALONZO. He undoubtedly has his reasons.

VINCENT PINZÓN. Father, somewhere it's said that a true friend is like that flaming sword that forms the last rampart of the just. Alonzo is the Admiral's sword . . .

ALONZO. Captain Pinzón, I should be happy to see you get back to your ship as quickly as possible.

VINCENT PINZÓN. (*softly*) I am at your command.

ALONZO. I will show you the way . . .

VINCENT PINZÓN. Do not take that trouble . . . Just be good enough to pay my respects to the Admiral, and to assure him of my allegiance. Tell him also that it is possible that I will have to see him soon, on a most urgent matter. Perhaps even this very night. Father, farewell.

He leaves.

Scene IV

ARENAS. A curious character . . .

ALONZO. I don't like that type of man.

63

ARENAS. He is intelligent. Too intelligent . . .

ALONZO. I detest that affectation of lightness, that need to make fun of everything constantly . . .

ARENAS. You don't like joy, Alonzo?

ALONZO. Pinzón's irony is not joy, Father. I would rather pity him, for he is not happy.

ARENAS. And you, Alonzo, you are happy?

ALONZO. I shall be the day we reach land.

ARENAS. You don't doubt our success then?

ALONZO. I don't doubt it. I have never doubted it.

ARENAS. I admire your certainty.

ALONZO. Without sharing it?

ARENAS. I have no opinion on this point. But I have one, alas, on the value of this success . . . (*a pause*) There exist victories, my son, which it is preferable not to win. For they make God himself suffer.

ALONZO. Think, Father, of the immensity of the lands to whom we shall bring the word of Christ.

ARENAS. Provided that we reach them in the name of Christ.

ALONZO. Since the time of the Apostles, no mission of this magnitude has been confided to men.

ARENAS. Is it really you who speak, my son? Behind your voice, I hear another . . . You love the Admiral so much?

ALONZO. Father, I admire his genius. I love his kindness. Everything I am I owe to him.

ARENAS. This makes my task more difficult and more painful than I had thought . . . But I must now express myself with total frankness. I must ask you to abandon this man.

ALONZO. Father!

ARENAS. As you would the greatest danger that can threaten your faith. (*a pause*) I am speaking to you as your confessor . . .

ALONZO. I do not . . .

ARENAS. I know that I astonish you.

ALONZO. More than that, Father! You . . . Excuse me! You make me doubt you . . .

ARENAS. I am happy, my son, that it is only I you doubted.

ALONZO. Will you at least give me an explanation? I think you owe me one.

ARENAS. I owe you one, you say? I thought you were more respectful of the rules of spiritual guidance! You must realize that to obey it is not absolutely necessary to understand.

ALONZO. In the present case . . .

ARENAS. In the present case, as in any other, I am the sole judge, in God's name, of what constitutes your salvation or your loss! (*a pause*) I am willing however to take into account the difficulty in which I find you, and to tell you what I know . . . My son, this man represents a greater danger for the Christian world than all the Moors of King Boabdil, for he hides his action under the appearance of faith. Yes, he constantly has the name of the Lord on his lips, but only to make Him serve his designs, his monstrous pride, the quenching of that thirst for knowledge which the devil who possesses him has placed in him to the peril of the world!

ALONZO. Father!

ARENAS. He makes fun of God, of all of us, and of you. India is all that is important to him! And yet it may not even be true . . . I fear that he attaches less importance to the discovery of a new world than to the new world that this discovery will cause to spring up in the minds of men!

ALONZO. Father, I beg you . . .

ARENAS. And I beg you to allow me to finish. When I think of this duplicity, I cannot hold back the anger that swells within me . . . It is as if Christ were drawn with words of love to a dark corner to be strangled.

ALONZO. (*supplicating*) I beg you . . .

ARENAS. (*becoming more and more excited*) Cursed be the children who will be born into a universe that will know the springtime of pride, into a world in which man will believe that he is God and will scoff at the faith of our age, in which sin, submerging priests, will push its poisoned head up through the ruins of holy places!

65

ALONZO. Passion is leading you astray, Father. You are mistaken
. . . The Admiral is an honest and pious man . . .

ARENAS. He is impious and sacrilegious.

ALONZO. The Church has not condemned him!

ARENAS. It will condemn those who follow him! (*a pause*) Do you,
or do you not, recognize my spiritual authority?

ALONZO. Today you are abusing it . . .

ARENAS. I exercise it for the salvation of the Church and for yours
as well. If you wish to avoid the punishment of the mutineers, it
is time for you to choose!

ALONZO. I do not fear death.

ARENAS. It is not of death that I speak. The interdict or excommunication will be ample punishment for you.

ALONZO. (*after a long pause*) What do you order me to do?

ARENAS. Break with him, abjure the errors that he has led you to
commit, confess them, execute the commandments which, through
my voice, the Holy Catholic, Apostolic, Roman Church gives you.
Are you ready?

ALONZO. (*after a long pause*) I beg you to grant me an hour in which
to reach my decision.

ARENAS. (*also pausing*) Very well. Come to my cabin in an hour. (*a
gesture from Alonzo*) Do you still have something to say to me?
Columbus appears at the door.

ALONZO. (*lowering his head*) Simply that you are tearing me apart.

ARENAS. I am sorry, my son. I shall pray for you.

Scene V

COLUMBUS. (*in a very low voice*) Go now . . .
*He stands aside from the door, which has remained open on the
falling night and the sound of the sea.*

ARENAS. (*to Alonzo*) Remember my words, my son, and may God
inspire you!
*He blesses him, goes to the door, closing it behind him. A long
pause. Columbus advances toward the table.*

Scene VI

COLUMBUS. (*softly*) Sit down . . . (*Alonzo falls sobbing to his knees, at the base of the chair. Columbus lights the lamp. Then he goes toward the porthole, turning his back on Alonzo*) Today we have sailed fifty leagues. Fifty leagues more. (*more curtly to Alonzo*) I said to sit down. I shall dictate the log.
Alonzo rises and sits down at the table. He opens a large notebook and takes up a pen.

ALONZO. I am ready, Admiral.

COLUMBUS. (*dictating*) Thursday, October 11 . . . Sailed west-south-west in a heavy sea. Weather calmed toward evening . . . Although the season is far advanced, the air remains as sweet to breathe as it is in April in Seville . . . Have fished out a carved piece of wood, some grasses, and a branch of thorn covered with red fruit that seems to have been freshly cut . . . In the course of last night, we heard many birds pass . . . However, in spite of all these signs which indicate, without a doubt, our imminent approach to land, the men continue to complain of the length of the journey, which they find intolerable. I have great difficulty in controlling them . . . I learned just now of a mutiny that was to break out tonight, with the purpose of making me captive . . . (*Alonzo lifts his head and stops writing*) . . . My faithful Alonzo himself . . .

ALONZO. (*rising suddenly*) No!

COLUMBUS. (*gently*) I heard everything, Alonzo.

ALONZO. Then you must know that I have not betrayed you!

COLUMBUS. Not yet . . .

ALONZO. Do you think that I would lend a hand to this plot?

COLUMBUS. I cannot permit myself to be duped by anyone, Alonzo . . . Not even by you.

ALONZO. I have placed my faith in you.

COLUMBUS. I am not God, Alonzo. Through the voice of this priest, He has ordered you to break with me. You must obey Him.

ALONZO. You are scorning me?

COLUMBUS. If I scorned you, I would allow you to choose . . .

Alonzo, I had selected you from among all the others to follow me and to continue my work. I love you enough to renounce this dream for the price of your peace. (*a pause*) Go find Arenas, and tell him that you are breaking with me . . .

ALONZO. No!

COLUMBUS. You would brave excommunication? (*a pause*) Be careful of your words, for they are going to bind you forever! . . .

ALONZO. (*after a long pause*) I don't know . . .

COLUMBUS. You see!

ALONZO. I beg your pardon.

COLUMBUS. I have nothing to pardon you for. The grace of God that we have received is not the same.

ALONZO. I am a coward . . .

COLUMBUS. But no, my boy, no . . . You stood up to him as best you could. He is a fearful adversary. (*a long pause*) By the way, you remember that a few weeks ago I gave you a letter? Do you still have it?

ALONZO. Yes.

COLUMBUS. (*softly*) Give it back to me, please.

ALONZO. But why?

COLUMBUS. I ask you to.

ALONZO. What's in the letter?

COLUMBUS. Some orders of no importance . . . Give it back to me, will you? (*Alonzo draws the letter from his doublet, and, after a final hesitation, holds it out to Columbus, who takes it casually and places it on the table*) Thank you . . . Now, my boy, I should like you to leave me a moment . . . I have work to do . . .

ALONZO. I do not wish to abandon you.

COLUMBUS. It's useless, Alonzo . . . You must.

ALONZO. I don't want to.

COLUMBUS. You must. You aren't made to bear the heavy burdens, to endure the long dreams, the hard days . . . For me revolt and solitude are my sisters! You would suffocate in the tumult in which they make me live.

ALONZO. I have only my devotion to offer you . . .

COLUMBUS. Devotion is not enough, Alonzo. (*a pause*) Even if this had not taken place, in six months, in a year, another enemy would have separated us. And one day, because you doubted yourself, you would begin to doubt me . . .

ALONZO. No . . .

COLUMBUS. To hate me, perhaps . . . No, Alonzo, I am responsible for you. And I don't want you to risk your soul any longer.

ALONZO. You certainly risk yours!

COLUMBUS. That is different. It is a great wager I made with God, and one I cannot free myself from. It is a wager I made by myself, alone, and which, alone, I must hold to.

ALONZO. Why do you want to justify my cowardice? Why cover it up with pretty words? The truth is simpler, and does me less honor. I believe in you. I believe in your mission. I know that God will see higher than this priest. But I am abandoning you at the first battle . . .

COLUMBUS. (*after a pause*) And if Arenas was right?

ALONZO. Is it really you who speak like that?

COLUMBUS. That's a question I ask myself. I may be mistaken, Alonzo . . . I may be completely mistaken. It is possible that I have been mistaken forever, and that truth is on the side of the contemptible, the envious, the ignorant. It may be that the earth is flat, and that India does not exist. It may also be impious to wish to reach it.

ALONZO. You do not believe what you are saying.

COLUMBUS. Chance has been so constant in sowing obstacles in my path that I come to wonder if Providence has not some part in it.

ALONZO. Only to greatly increase your merit . . .

COLUMBUS. Or to turn me from my object . . . This time, destiny has better chosen its emissary. It no longer strikes directly . . . I astonish you, Alonzo?

ALONZO. This admission of your uncertainty . . .

COLUMBUS. (*becoming more and more passionate*) I have never made that admission to you, have I? I don't think I've ever made it to myself . . . All my life, Alonzo, I have repeated the same cry, the same monotonous cry, like the bird that has only one

69

note in its throat. How could I hear my own sighs? From year to year, from city to city, from castle to castle, I have been this absurd prophet, dressed in rags and wearing a dunce cap, whom the servants chase through the kitchens, drive with blows toward the ditch, and who, under all the insults and rubbish hurled at him, can only bow his head repeating his one cry: "India! India! India!" Who knows whether or not the servants did not show as much understanding as their masters? (*a short pause*) What is the matter, Alonzo? Why do you tremble? Are you afraid?

ALONZO. It wasn't enough for you to lose me? You must still . . .

COLUMBUS. Still what? . . . Go on. Go on then! . . .

ALONZO. You must still disturb me deeply.

COLUMBUS. Disturb you? Are you disturbed or do you doubt, perhaps? You doubt, do you not?

ALONZO. No.

COLUMBUS. Yes . . . Admit it. You, in your turn, doubt me . . .

ALONZO. Please.

COLUMBUS. Do you know that I could furnish you ten good reasons to convince you again? Ten good reasons, each one of which is as good as the other? Do you know that?

ALONZO. (*quickly*) Yes . . .

COLUMBUS. Listen then, you man of little faith! Listen to the reasons of this madman who speaks to you. Listen to these reasons that he sings to himself to rock himself to sleep, like a mad woman who rocks her dead babe . . . Listen then, man in whom I believed. Two years ago, when, on the conclusions of Talavera, the commission of experts presented its report unfavorable to the expedition that I proposed, this voice, which, in spite of the gibes of the scholars and geographers, convinced the Queen, this voice which silenced the opposition and made my cause triumph, this voice, was it not the voice of God?

ALONZO. (*in the same tone of voice*) Yes . . .

COLUMBUS. (*advancing slowly toward Alonzo*) And that day when our ships were immobilized on a sea so calm that the sailors feared never being able to advance any more, He who made the waves to rise and the sails to swell without any sign having announced Him, was that not God?

ALONZO. (*recoiling before Columbus*) Yes . . . yes . . .

COLUMBUS. (*in the same tone of voice*) And that other day, when the crew threatened to rise up in its entirety against me, He who sent that white bird that you brought me, was that not God?

ALONZO. (*in the same tone*) Yes . . . yes . . .

COLUMBUS. (*pausing*) You see . . . You are easily convinced . . . Now, get out.

ALONZO. I beg you . . .

COLUMBUS. Get out! (*shouting*) Get out!

Alonzo, who is still not far from the door, flees. Columbus, who has remained alone, rushes to the table, seizes the letter that Alonzo has given him, tears it up in rage, and throws the pieces on the floor. He rubs his hand across his forehead, staggers forward, and stops in the middle of the room, his back turned to the crucifix.

Scene VII

COLUMBUS. (*whispering*) Now, O Lord, I have nothing more to offer you . . . Nothing more to offer you.
Darkness. Followed immediately by

THIRD TABLEAU

The deck of the Santa Maria, *one hour after the preceding tableau.*

A VOICE.

Yes, it seems to be a night like all the others . . . The wind rose a bit during the day, but now all is calm. The sea is quiet. There is not a single star. And the darkness is so deep that it is impossible to see more than a few steps. Even the whiteness of the folded sail at the foot of the mast makes a spot that is scarcely whiter . . .

All the sailors are finally asleep, with the exception of those two over there who continue to whisper to each other. No sound can be heard, except for the creaking of the hull as it rests its weight in the wave, the strain on the anchor chain, and that multitude of drops that it brings forth from the water, in the crackle of a brief and sudden swell.

Columbus is still in his cabin, and Vincent Pinzón has started out to join him.

Yes, it is a night that seems to be like all the others.

And yet, this time, land is so close! So close that the song of a bird, that the cry of a child on the shore, could almost be heard on board. The prow of the *Santa Maria*, which precedes a little the two other ships, has stopped less than a mile from the island. If the lookout could see through the darkness, he would notice the foliage of the large trees, whose branches are gently moving in the trade winds . . . But he, too, has tired of waiting, and sleeps.

What a silence, suddenly, at the heart of the world. Now God leans over the earth. The time has come to knot up what was unknotted, to unite what had been separate.

Then God chooses a man on the island. He awakes him. He guides his steps toward the beach. And there He shows him three lights that shine on the waves, the flight of two arrows' distance away, three lights that shine on the waves, and remain motionless.

Then the man that God has chosen lights a torch. He raises it above his head, as high as he can, and swings it from left to right, from right to left, to greet the spirit which has come upon the waters.

Darkness. Followed immediately by

FOURTH TABLEAU

Columbus's cabin. As the curtain rises, the Admiral is alone, op-posite a porthole, in an attitude of great attention. He turns his back to the door. Vincent Pinzón appears at the door. He hesitates a moment before coming in. Columbus does not turn around at once.

COLUMBUS. Come in, Vincent . . .

VINCENT PINZÓN. You were expecting me?

COLUMBUS. *(turning toward Vincent)* Yes.

VINCENT PINZÓN. Alonzo told you I was coming?

COLUMBUS. It wasn't necessary. From the chart room, one can hear everything that is said here.

VINCENT PINZÓN. Ah! *(a pause)* And you listened?

COLUMBUS. I have no pride when my goal is at stake.

VINCENT PINZÓN. I have nothing more to apprise you of. I ask your pardon for having uselessly disobeyed your orders . . . *(He starts toward the door)*

COLUMBUS. *(softly)* Stay, Vincent . . . I am very grateful to you.

VINCENT PINZÓN. I have done what I thought I should do.

COLUMBUS. I know.

VINCENT PINZÓN. May I ask what arrangements you have made?

COLUMBUS. None.

VINCENT PINZÓN. *(astonished)* You intend to allow them to climb on board?

COLUMBUS. They will not come on board.

VINCENT PINZÓN. I'm afraid you don't know Martin Pinzón, Admiral.

COLUMBUS. I am going to make a prediction, Vincent. But this time I shall not glory in my clairvoyance. In an hour — why, yes — in five minutes, the men who are now my most militant adversaries will become my most servile courtiers. All of them, your brother included . . . All! All, except one perhaps . . .

VINCENT PINZÓN. What do you mean?

COLUMBUS. Go to that porthole, Vincent! Look, look carefully. And tell me what you see . . . *(Without replying, Vincent Pinzón goes to the porthole and looks out. Columbus, who has not moved, turns his back on him. After a moment, Vincent turns suddenly toward Columbus)* What do you see, Vincent?

VINCENT PINZÓN. I see a light shining.

73

COLUMBUS. Describe it . . .

VINCENT PINZÓN. It looks like a poor wax candle. I see it rise and fall, as if it followed the rhythmic step of a man walking in the night . . .

COLUMBUS. That is exactly what I thought I saw.

VINCENT PINZÓN. There is no more than a mile between it and us.

COLUMBUS. No more than a mile, in fact . . .

VINCENT PINZÓN. (*turning toward Columbus*) So? . . .

COLUMBUS. (*slowly*) Yes, Vincent. The goal has been reached.

VINCENT PINZÓN. (*excitedly*) And you stand there like that? You must notify . . . (*He goes quickly toward the door*)

COLUMBUS. Why? What has waited for so many centuries can't wait a moment longer?

VINCENT PINZÓN. I don't understand you . . . You seem so joyless.

COLUMBUS. (*becoming more and more passionate*) Do you think so? Ah, Vincent! How poorly you know me! Is my joy to go prove to these hundred twenty cowards that they were mistaken, and enjoy the spectacle of their open mouths, their trembling jaws? . . . No . . . At this moment that God has given me, I want to remain alone. Alone, as I have always been! Who has not shared my agony will not share my joy! He who has not known with me the spit, the filth, and the rod, cannot grasp with me the course of the world. All my life, Vincent, is in this moment . . . If it does not exist, then I have not existed! If this light were suddenly to go out, God has mocked me! But it shines, Vincent, it shines! And Columbus is finally face to face with Columbus. Face to face with Columbus, the wretched, the baffled, beaten madman, for one moment now stands Columbus, the man of God. And you would have me miss that confrontation? . . . Go join the others, Vincent, go join them, and watch their faces. (*a pause*) Go . . . You will have them sing the "Gloria." (*As Vincent starts to leave, the voice of the lookout can be heard, crying "Land!" and, soon afterward, like an echo, the same cry is repeated by the lookouts on the other ships. A noise on the deck. Cannon shot.*) Do you hear? The *Pinta's* cannon! . . .

The noise increases. A second cannon shot.

VINCENT PINZÓN. The *Niña!*

COLUMBUS. Now, leave me, Vincent . . . I turn over my command to you for tonight . . . We shall land at dawn.

Vincent Pinzón runs out. A sudden silence. Columbus remains alone, gazing at the crucifix.

CURTAIN

CHARLES BERTIN

DON JUAN

translated by William Jay Smith

———∞———

Stolen waters are sweet, and bread
eaten in secret is pleasant.
But he knoweth not that the dead are
there; and that her guests are in the
depths of hell.

Proverbs 9: 17, 18

CHARACTERS

Donna Laura da Risino (28 years old)
Don Manuel La Mota (44 years old)
Donna Mencia da Ravallo (32 years old)
Isabella, an Italian Duchess (29 years old)
Don Juan Tenorio (38 years old)
Octavio, an Italian duke, Isabella's fiancé
    (37 years old)
Giacomo, Octavio's friend
Doña Anne de Ulloa (18 years old)
Pepita, Isabella's maid
Mamita, Anne's nurse (60 years old)
Belisa, Anne's maid
Don Gonzalo de Ulloa, Commander of Seville,
    Anne's father (50 years old)

Act I

The scene represents a salon adjoining the ballroom in the palace of the King of Naples. Upstage, two windows open on a star-filled night. On the garden side, a door opens on to the palace park. Muffled music may be heard in the background. On the court side, another door separates the scene from the ballroom. When this door is opened, the music enters along with the characters. Furniture of the period. A little divan. Thick, full-length curtains. A few candelabra, giving only half light.

Scene I

When the curtain rises, Laura stands alone. La Mota enters immediately from the ballroom. Laura runs to meet him.

LAURA. Did you see him? What did he say? (*La Mota is dumbfounded and silent*) Tell me what he said. (*La Mota still does not answer*) I implore you! . . . Tell me!

LA MOTA. He refuses to speak to you, Signora.

LAURA. (*softly*) Ah! (*a pause*) Tell me what he said!

LA MOTA. Must I?

LAURA. You must.

LA MOTA. He says that the night is made for dancing, and not for weeping.

LAURA. And what else? . . .

LA MOTA. (*reluctantly*) He says there are other men in Naples.

LAURA. (*gives a start, then pauses*) Do you think . . . Do you think . . . those are his final words?

LA MOTA. I fear so, Signora.

A pause.

LAURA. La Mota, you are his friend.

LA MOTA. If it is possible to be Don Juan's friend, yes, Signora, I am his friend.

LAURA. Will you try again? He will listen to you perhaps. I am . . . I am . . . (*She hides her face in her hands*)

La Mota bows without replying and starts to leave as Mencia enters.

Scene II

MENCIA. Ah, here you are at last, La Mota! I've been looking everywhere for you. But I seem to be intruding. Are you by chance paying court to our dear Laura? No? Then, come dance! . . .

LA MOTA. (*curtly*) Excuse me . . . (*He leaves abruptly*)

Scene III

MENCIA. (*approaching Laura*) I'm terribly sorry, my dear, to have broken in on you like this . . . But now that I have, may I sit down?

LAURA. (*startled*) But, of course . . .

MENCIA. I should not want to disturb you . . .

LAURA. Please . . .

MENCIA. (*sitting down*) Don't you find that it's stifling here? I'm literally suffocating. Of course, I haven't stopped dancing . . . You don't enjoy dancing, Donna Laura?

LAURA. No . . . Not tonight . . . I . . . It's really so warm.

MENCIA. I didn't see you in the ballroom, and I wondered if you were feeling ill. You aren't, are you?

LAURA. No. I feel quite well, thank you.

MENCIA. Excuse my curiosity. But such a change is most astonishing . . . You danced so much the other evening.

LAURA. I don't remember.

MENCIA. You don't remember? You have forgotten last month's ball at the Governor's? (*a pause*) The ball given to celebrate the arrival in Naples of the envoy of the King of Spain, Don Juan Tenorio. Now you remember, don't you? (*a pause*) You were seen with him quite often . . . Not with the Governor, of course. With Don Juan . . .

LAURA. (*slowly*) Yes. He dances well.

MENCIA. You insult him. He dances better than well. He dances ravishingly. And, what is more, he "ravishes" a great deal, doesn't he?

LAURA. (*with some effort*) So I am told.

MENCIA. All talk is of his conquests. This evening, he has not left the side of Donna Isabella. Tongues are already wagging.

LAURA. (*curtly*) So it seems.

MENCIA. They say that tonight isn't the first time that they have danced together . . . and also . . . that they dance elsewhere, less fully clothed. It is true that it is awfully warm! I must say I understand them . . . But Octavio will perhaps not understand. And if he learns that his fiancée does not always dance in public, I fear that he may give a few saber thrusts at the orchestra . . .

LAURA. Will you stop, please! I am . . . I am so tired. (*She sinks into a chair, her head in her hands*)

MENCIA. Excuse me, Laura. I'm boring you with all this nonsense . . . But is it my fault if the world is made that way? One woman weeps because she loves too much, another because she is not in love, and both because they are not loved! You, at least, have been loved . . . For a while, anyway . . . which is better than nothing. (*A pause. Mencia approaches Laura and leans over her*) You may rest assured, Laura, I am not a rival . . . I hate Don Juan and everything that he touches. I hate this man who is idolized by the most exquisite women. And I don't understand the delirium which takes hold of all of you the moment he appears . . . But I can at least give you a piece of advice . . . Love him less, and you will keep him. Look at Donna Isabella: a short while ago, she could have given lessons in virtue to the entire court. Today, look at her! She picks up his handkerchiefs! She is His Lordship's servant . . . Just wait: in one month, she will be where you are . . .

Isabella enters on these words.

ISABELLA. (*curtly to Mencia*) Leave us . . .

Mencia bows ironically to Isabella and leaves. Laura draws herself up on seeing Isabella, and faces her.

Scene IV

ISABELLA. (*softly*) They told me you wanted to talk to me, Laura . . .

LAURA. That's not true! It's . . .

ISABELLA. So it's Don Juan you wish to see.

LAURA. Indeed. But not with you.

ISABELLA. This is my home, Laura. He will see you in my presence . . . or not at all.

LAURA. The envoy of His Catholic Majesty will certainly appreciate your attention to protocol!

ISABELLA. As long as he is under my roof, I shall make every effort to keep people from annoying him. (*a pause*) What do you want of him?

LAURA. I do not have to answer to you for anything.

ISABELLA. I admire your discretion. I wish that it were always so exemplary.

LAURA. What do you mean?

ISABELLA. I mean that it would be desirable to give less rein to a feeling which your glances, your sighs, and your tears reveal to the whole city.

LAURA. And you give me that order.

ISABELLA. Not order — advice.

LAURA. From Spain?

ISABELLA. From me.

LAURA. I'm grateful for your solicitude, Isabella. But I don't think that Don Juan's mistress is in a position to dictate my conduct.

ISABELLA. You forget to whom you speak.

LAURA. Your Grace must forgive me. I am speaking to the fiancée

82

of Octavio, to that same Isabella who dared to remind me, just a moment ago, to respect convention.

ISABELLA. Signora, I understand that you have a palazzo in Florence. The time has come for you to retire to it.

LAURA. More advice?

ISABELLA. This time, it is an order.

LAURA. Which of us, Isabella, will leave Naples first?

ISABELLA. You. And in an hour! (*She turns around brusquely and steps quickly toward the door*)

LAURA. You are going to see the King? (*Isabella stops*) Remember that you will have to tell him everything. Everything. For I am going with you . . .

She also steps forward and joins Isabella, who sinks into a chair.

ISABELLA. Very well. What do you want of me?

LAURA. I told you. I want to see Juan. Alone. He's coming to join you here, isn't he?

ISABELLA. And if he should?

LAURA. You will tell him that I'll be waiting for him. Tonight.

ISABELLA. And if he has another rendezvous?

As the two women confront each other, the door of the ballroom opens and Don Juan appears with La Mota. Laura, in a corner of the room, has time to hide behind one of the long curtains. Isabella rises.

Scene V

DON JUAN. Isabella . . . I was looking for you.

ISABELLA. And you have found me, Juan.

DON JUAN. (*to La Mota*) La Mota, will you tell His Majesty that I have been called away . . . (*He looks at Isabella*) . . . on urgent business . . . (*He approaches her, addressing her more tenderly*) on the most urgent business?

La Mota, who has remained at the door, leaves. Don Juan takes Isabella in his arms and kisses her.

ISABELLA. Do you sometimes mean what you say, Juan?

DON JUAN. Always, Isabella, always . . . Do you doubt it? (*He*

83

turns from her and takes a few steps, carefully inspecting the room. He glances toward the curtain that hides Laura)

ISABELLA. What are you doing?

DON JUAN. The earth is covered with those, my dear, who spy on our happiness . . .

ISABELLA. Because they envy it . . . Let us pity them.

DON JUAN. You are very generous.

ISABELLA. And you are very prudent.

DON JUAN. I am not prudent, Isabella, but curious . . . I show as much interest in those who hate me as in those who love me . . . Just think that all that is needed is a cupboard, a half-opened door, a curtain to hide a husband, a fiancé, or a vengeful mistress . . . By the slightest inattention, Isabella, you might see cut off before your very eyes the thread of a noble life . . .

ISABELLA. Don't joke, Juan.

DON JUAN. And why shouldn't I joke, Isabella?

ISABELLA. I might be that woman, one day . . .

DON JUAN. You would kill me.

ISABELLA. I'd be capable of it.

DON JUAN. Really?

ISABELLA. I love you, Juan, for better or for worse. Instruct me then, so that I may know how you will abandon me. Shall I receive a bouquet of Spanish roses and a diamond like the others?

DON JUAN. You have heard that?

ISABELLA. Yes. And that sometimes the diamond was returned. But never the roses.

DON JUAN. What stupid things are attributed to me, Isabella. I hope you don't believe them?

ISABELLA. I don't know, Juan. I'm so afraid that after the torture of having won you there may be the other interminable torture of losing you. That I would find unbearable.

DON JUAN. Nothing is unbearable.

ISABELLA. You don't understand, Juan. If you abandon me, I shall die.

DON JUAN. Great words, Isabella. And words out of place in a ballroom. (*He sits down on the divan*) Come, sit beside me . . . Come . . .

ISABELLA. Yes, Juan. (*A pause. She sits down next to him*)

DON JUAN. So . . . All is well. (*A pause. To himself*) Stolen waters are sweet, and bread eaten in secret is pleasant . . .

ISABELLA. What did you say?

DON JUAN. Nothing . . .

ISABELLA. Are you happy, Juan?

DON JUAN. Is that necessary, Isabella? I've told you that all is well . . . What more do you want?

ISABELLA. Nothing, Juan. To look at your face . . . When you sleep, you have the same expression on your face. The look of a defenseless child. And at night you nestle against me as if you were seeking a refuge . . .

DON JUAN. I don't like people to watch me sleep.

ISABELLA. I need to watch you, Juan. That is the only moment when you are really mine.

DON JUAN. (*rising*) Must you, Isabella? You are certainly in a strange mood this evening . . . What is the matter?

A short pause. Isabella also rises.

ISABELLA. Nothing.

DON JUAN. Yes, there is. Tell me. (*Isabella sadly shrugs her shoulders*) Who has been speaking to you?

ISABELLA. No one, Juan.

DON JUAN. (*very tenderly*) You can lie, too, Isabella? I thought that privilege was reserved to me. (*a pause*) You've nothing to say? (*a longer pause*) As you like . . . Then I'll speak. I think that you asked me if I would leave you one day. The answer is yes.

ISABELLA. Juan!

DON JUAN. A time will come, Isabella, when I shall discover another light in other eyes, another smile on other lips, when I shall notice that there are other women on this earth, whose bodies look deceptively like yours . . .

ISABELLA. Juan!

DON JUAN. A time will come, Isabella, when your beauty will seem insipid, your grace all affectation. You will weep, Isabella!

85

ISABELLA. Juan, have mercy!

DON JUAN. You will implore me, Isabella. And I shall calmly reject you. You will be unhappy, Isabella. And I shall laugh with other women at your suffering.

ISABELLA. Juan, oh, Juan!

DON JUAN. You will lose all pride, all modesty . . . You will spy on me. You will watch my glances, my smiles, my gestures. (*He moves slowly toward the spot where Laura is hidden*) And perhaps you will hide in the dark to be present at my rendezvous like the proud, noble Donna Laura da Risino. (*He draws the curtain hiding Laura*) You see, Isabella, that your discretion was useless: I noticed the Signora as soon as I came in. You know each other, I take it? . . .

LAURA. Don Juan, you will be punished one day!

DON JUAN. So I have often been warned, Signora. But for the moment, I am very well.

LAURA. You are disgusting.

DON JUAN. (*tenderly*) Will you tell me that one day, Isabella? (*A pause. Isabella remains silent. Curtly*) Or will you tell me now perhaps? What do you think of that? Answer me. (*Isabella is silent*) Am I what this woman says I am? (*curtly*) Answer me!

ISABELLA. (*begging*) Please, Juan . . .

DON JUAN. (*with a terrible tenderness*) Your opinion on the subject would interest me greatly, Isabella.

ISABELLA. No, Juan, you are not disgusting. You are . . .

DON JUAN. I am? . . .

ISABELLA. You are unfortunate.

DON JUAN. You think so? (*turning to Laura*) Well, Signora, you wanted to see me. Here I am . . .

LAURA. You are vile, Don Juan.

DON JUAN. I see that we must exchange the traditional banalities.

LAURA. You are despicable . . . Nothing is sacred to you. Nothing counts for you, except yourself and your dirty little pleasures . . .

DON JUAN. Which were also yours, Signora. I remember that not so long ago, you shared them with all your heart.

LAURA. I loved you, I would have given up everything for you, if you had asked me. I would have killed for you! I would have sacrificed my soul for you . . . my husband, my children!

DON JUAN. I don't understand you, Signora. A love like that need not be requited . . . It is so great that I scarcely exist beside it. You must be very happy.

LAURA. Before knowing you, I thought so. But you have destroyed everything . . . For your three weeks of pleasure. To add a name in the little book that you once showed me. I hate you, I hate you . . .

DON JUAN. (*with pretended admiration*) Perfect, Laura! How naturally and simply you put it! "I hate you!" How splendidly you pronounce those words. (*changing his tone*) . . . Now it's my turn . . . Have I broken one of my promises, Signora? Did I swear love and fidelity? Certainly not. There are words whose use I guard carefully for some improbable and marvelous occasion! They are too beautiful to be ruined. All we promised each other was pleasure. We had it. That is all.

ISABELLA. (*with pent-up anger*) Stop this silly business, Juan!

DON JUAN. Did I tell you that I loved you?

ISABELLA. No, Juan.

DON JUAN. You are sure?

ISABELLA. Yes.

DON JUAN. For the simple reason that I don't love you, either, Isabella, unfortunate though that may be! (*turning toward Laura*) As for you, Laura, I should find it most agreeable if you would leave me alone from now on. (*in a harsh, low voice*) Now, the scene is over, finished. You've uttered your last words. We have nothing more to say to each other.

LAURA. Very well, then. It will be as you have wished.

She runs out across the park. A long pause. Don Juan goes to the windows.

Scene VI

DON JUAN. What a lovely night. One would think that the earth had stopped breathing . . . The birds themselves are silent . . .

And yet this evening the woods are filled with lovers: if we walked down the paths, we would hear their sighs. What a strange thing love is, Isabella. Two beings meet, look at each other, draw from that look what strange certainty. And then suddenly they are linked in the most extraordinary solidarity in the world. They pretend that they share everything, their belongings, their meals, their bed, and even their souls. As if one could share one's soul. Don't you find that idea absurd?

ISABELLA. Which idea, Juan?

DON JUAN. That one can share one's soul?

ISABELLA. No.

DON JUAN. Like an orange.

ISABELLA. No, Juan. I don't find it absurd. On the contrary, it's a very simple thing.

DON JUAN. Poor Octavio.

ISABELLA. Why?

DON JUAN. How inconsistent you are, Isabella! You prefer me to your fiancé, and then you wonder why I pity him. (*a pause*) But you are right: I do not pity him because of that. I'm just afraid that he will die tonight.

ISABELLA. What do you mean, Juan?

DON JUAN. Where do you think Signora da Risino ran when she left? (*a pause*) She went to warn Octavio that we were together. And you'll soon see him rush here with one or two of his friends, his sword in hand.

ISABELLA. Then, let's leave, Juan. Let's leave! . . .

DON JUAN. That's quite impossible, Isabella. I have committed the greatest possible offense against that man: I have taken his fiancée. And you want me to flee the just reparation that I owe him? No, no, he will be satisfied . . . and will die by no other hand than mine. This very night . . . Pray for him, Isabella!

ISABELLA. You are mad, Juan! And if he killed you?

DON JUAN. That is out of the question, my dear. I have no intention of dying so soon. I still have many nights to spend with you.

ISABELLA. So many, Juan?

DON JUAN. Quite . . . I must see you still many times brushing your hair and tying your ribbons. I must see you many mornings wake up in my arms not knowing whether or not I shall love you, Isabella. (*a short pause*) Or whether I shall remember, as I do of other women, only the warmth of your body and the sweetness of your skin.

Octavio and Giacomo enter on these words. They remain at the door, Octavio standing a little ahead of Giacomo. Don Juan sees them and slowly embraces Isabella, while Octavio's companion places his hand on his friend's arm to hold him back. Then Don Juan advances slowly toward them.

Scene VII

DON JUAN. You were looking for me, gentlemen?

OCTAVIO. I am looking for the man for whom Hell gapes, the man who fouls and damns all that he touches, the man . . .

DON JUAN. If you mean me, I am ready to answer to you.

OCTAVIO. I have always drawn my sword for you, Isabella — each time you have been insulted. I did not realize that this time you consented to the insult.

ISABELLA. I implore you, Octavio, in the name of the love that you had for me: don't fight! It's stupid! It's useless.

OCTAVIO. It's useless to ask me not to, Signora. I have only one regret, and that's soiling my sword with this man's blood.

DON JUAN. You are eloquent, Signor. Rest assured that your sword will remain pure. It may be buried with you, for it will not touch me.

ISABELLA. Juan, don't fight.

DON JUAN. I am sorry, my dear. But I have the deepest respect for the protocol of honor. I am pleased to fight with this gentleman. And you, in spite of all you say, would think little of me if I were to flee.

ISABELLA. You don't know then that I love you.

DON JUAN. Ah, how maladroit, Isabella! Don't you see you are putting Octavio in a rage, and that you've made a cutting remark, worse than those we made to each other a few minutes ago. For

89

you see since his majestic entrance, all we've done is exchange cutting remarks. But this is all according to protocol. Before every duel, one must work oneself into a rage by hurling carefully chosen insults at one's opponent. The Ancients always did that. And you might well be some modern Sabina . . .

OCTAVIO. I await you, Signor.

ISABELLA. (*throwing herself toward him*) Have pity, Octavio! . . .

OCTAVIO. (*curtly*) I am sorry, Signora.

DON JUAN. Now, it is I who await you, Signor. I shall be at the main gate. (*turning to Isabella*) I'll see you soon, Isabella. I am going to tell my friend La Mota, who is probably strolling in the park; he will keep you company during my absence. I shall not be long. (*He leaves with Giacomo.*)

Scene VIII

ISABELLA. Octavio!

OCTAVIO. No, Isabella. I love you enough to place your honor above mine. But even if I behaved like a coward to please you, I would still have to avenge the insult that you have received.

ISABELLA. No one has insulted me. I am his with my full consent.

OCTAVIO. So you think, Signora. I remember another Isabella, who graciously swore her troth to me.

ISABELLA. That was indeed another Isabella, Octavio. Oh, don't think that I enjoy torturing you. I say it because it's true, simply because it's true. I know that I've treated you badly, that you have suffered, and that you are still suffering. But I beg you to believe me that I am neither harsh nor cruel. I could not act otherwise. It is as if . . .

OCTAVIO. As if you had changed worlds.

ISABELLA. Yes, Octavio. I look at you and recognize you. I know what you have been for me. But you are so distant, a thousand leagues from me . . . You must understand me. God knows that I am not evil. I have simply become a stranger to all my past life.

OCTAVIO. You have forgotten many things, Isabella.

90

ISABELLA. I have the feeling of having learned everything, Octavio.

OCTAVIO. You have learned sin.

ISABELLA. I am pure of all sin: I love him. You do not understand. Oh, I know I have betrayed you in the eyes of men, I have paraded my immodesty, I have behaved like a courtesan. Now, I am torturing you. But deep within me, very deep within me, there is . . .

OCTAVIO. There is?

ISABELLA. There is the certainty that God sees me and approves of me.

OCTAVIO. You are blasphemous.

ISABELLA. Sin, Octavio, is all that one commits without love. Law without love, righteousness without love, virtue without love are also sins. I soil myself in your eyes. But for God, I am pure. It was before knowing this debauchee that I sinned, Octavio.

OCTAVIO. I pity you, Isabella.

ISABELLA. (*with a great outburst of feeling*) I am happy. I love him. This is no longer a phrase that I have on my lips, or even in my heart. It is a way of living, of breathing, of touching wood, of looking at a face, of opening my window in the morning, of welcoming things that come. Even if he died, even if he left me, Octavio, no one could take back from me what he has given me. Ah, how I should like to express what is happening within me. Then you would know that I have not betrayed you by leaving. The woman you knew has died loving you as she could love you. Another woman has been born in her place, one who has perhaps the same face, but who is as different from her as she is from any woman in the world.

OCTAVIO. Perhaps. But I have not changed. The gift of myself that I made you one day I made to the Isabella you were and to all those you might become. (*a pause*) Do you remember the day of our betrothal? That was a year ago next week.

ISABELLA. Yes, Octavio. How far away it seems!

OCTAVIO. Only one year ago, Isabella. (*a pause*) We had taken a boat out on the bay.

ISABELLA. Yes.

OCTAVIO. Do you remember, a storm came up.

ISABELLA. Yes, and I was not afraid.

OCTAVIO. You slipped your hand in mine. And you told me I was like the boat that held us both . . .

ISABELLA. Yes, Octavio.

OCTAVIO. Then I swore to you that I loved you. You looked at me without answering. But you ordered the oarsmen to cease their struggle against the storm. You told them to let the boat go its way, that you had confidence in it.

ISABELLA. I remember . . .

OCTAVIO. Arriving back in port, you said to me: "I give myself up to you, Octavio, just as I gave myself up to that boat."

ISABELLA. Forgive me! . . .

A long silence. Giacomo appears at the door.

GIACOMO. It is time, Octavio. Your opponent is waiting.

OCTAVIO. I'm coming, Giacomo.

ISABELLA. (*screaming*) I beg you, Octavio.

OCTAVIO. It's the only thing I cannot grant you, Isabella.

ISABELLA. I swear to you that if you kill him, I shall die.

OCTAVIO. (*after a long pause*) Perhaps he will kill me . . . (*a pause*) Farewell, Isabella. Forgive me for having taken so long to understand you.

ISABELLA. You cannot understand me, Octavio . . .

OCTAVIO. Who knows? (*a pause*) I shall always love you. May God keep you!

He leaves. A long pause.

ISABELLA. A boat, a boat indeed . . . He is more like the sea itself!
She remains alone for a moment. Then La Mota enters.

Scene IX

LA MOTA. My respects, Signora.

ISABELLA. Good evening, Señor La Mota.

LA MOTA. Don Juan has asked me to keep you company while we wait . . . But if you prefer to remain alone . . .

ISABELLA. No. Stay, Señor. I could not bear to be alone now. (*a pause*) God grant that he not be wounded!

LA MOTA. He has never been, Signora.

ISABELLA. Why are they fighting?

LA MOTA. Because they are gentlemen.

ISABELLA. It's absurd.

LA MOTA. Don Juan has fought more than fifty duels. You need fear nothing for him.

ISABELLA. I admire your calm . . .

LA MOTA. I assure you that he isn't in the slightest danger.

ISABELLA. Where are they?

LA MOTA. In the woods beside the sea just outside the park.

ISABELLA. (*walking up and down*) Oh!

LA MOTA. Please listen to me, Signora! The danger is not where you fear it: there is another one that is far more formidable! If something untoward happened to the Duke, we would have to leave Naples this very night, Juan and I . . .

ISABELLA. Leave Naples?

LA MOTA. The Duke enjoys the King's protection, you know. His death would be avenged pitilessly . . .

ISABELLA. Then, I will accompany you . . .

LA MOTA. Weigh your words, Signora. If you leave, what will people say? To flee is to admit your liaison with Don Juan. And His Majesty . . .

ISABELLA. (*interrupting him*) Never, I will never give up Juan, La Mota!

LA MOTA. The kingdom will be forbidden to you forever. You will lose your lands, your palaces.

ISABELLA. That will make no difference to me.

LA MOTA. Do you think that Don Juan will accept this sacrifice?

ISABELLA. It is not a sacrifice. Exile would be here without him. (*a pause*) Where will you go?

LA MOTA. I believe that we shall take refuge in Seville; my uncle is commander of that city. If you come with us, my cousin, Doña Anne de Ulloa, will look after you . . .

ISABELLA. I thank you.

LA MOTA. Did Juan speak to you of her?

ISABELLA. He told me that you were in love with her.

LA MOTA. That is true. You will perhaps smile when you see us together . . . She is eighteen, and I am forty-four.

ISABELLA. I never smile at the love of others. (*a pause*) He should be here by now! (*She goes toward the window, looks deep into the park, returns, walks up and down*)

LA MOTA. Calm yourself, Signora! (*At a sign of impatience from Isabella, La Mota in turn goes to the windows*) I see him. He is alone!

Isabella rushes to the window, then looks toward the door. Don Juan enters. She rushes to greet him.

ISABELLA. Juan! You are not wounded?

DON JUAN. No, I am not wounded.

ISABELLA. Octavio?

DON JUAN. (*with a sad shrug*) I should have liked to spare him, but he wouldn't let me. He fought very strangely indeed. First hesitantly, then with rage. Then, suddenly, with a nonchalance bordering on resignation. I thought him the better swordsman. It was a game . . . (*Isabella has sunk to the floor, her head in her hands, during these words. A pause*) It is strange. For a moment I had the impression that he did not want to kill me. And yet, when I gave him the final blow, he gathered all his energy to strike me once more. It almost seemed as if he wanted us to die together, like two old friends . . . (*a pause*) You have nothing to say, Isabella? (*a pause*) One must look this death in the face, as he has done. He died because of us, because of you . . . (*a pause*) You will bear that cross, Isabella.

A long pause. Isabella raises her head.

ISABELLA. You are the only cross that I shall ever bear, my love.

CURTAIN

Act II

The scene is laid in Isabella's apartments in the palace that she occupies in Seville.

Scene I

LA MOTA. Tomorrow it will be three months since we had that conversation in Naples. Do you recall it, Signora?

ISABELLA. Yes. It seems to me that it was yesterday. How short happiness is!

LA MOTA. You aren't happy?

ISABELLA. I am afraid, La Mota. I can feel misfortune approaching me like a beast in the shadows. It prowls. It watches me. It is still hiding, but at the first sign of weakness, it will leap on me. And all will be over!

LA MOTA. You will defend yourself.

ISABELLA. Certainly! But I have already struggled so much. I am tired, my friend, tired. Exhausted! And this time, I feel the danger is greater.

LA MOTA. It is always the same danger.

ISABELLA. I don't think so. I have already accepted so many of his whims, his daily infidelities. Because I knew that he would return to me. But today, I am afraid.

LA MOTA. Who is it?

ISABELLA. I don't know. That is precisely what troubles me. I don't know the name of the woman who will steal him from me. But somewhere she exists. And I am sure that he already knows her.

LA MOTA. I swear to you that he has told me nothing.

ISABELLA. Yet I know that I am not mistaken. I am beginning to know him. I have never seen a tiger ready to leap, but he must be like that. He concentrates. He draws in upon himself. He is handsomer, darker than ever. His eyes! . . . I can't see anything but danger in them. When he looks at me, he looks through me, without seeing me. If he speaks to me, it is with unusual gentleness. I'm waiting for the moment when that gentleness will change into anger, scorn, disgust. And I don't know what to say. It's terrible to know that whatever step I take will be the wrong one.

LA MOTA. Yes . . .

ISABELLA. (*without hearing him*) The first days in Naples, I thought that he loved me. He was so gentle. He questioned me incessantly, interpreted my slightest gesture or smile, trembled at the thought of my escaping him. He seemed to feed on no other anxiety than to know if I, too, loved him. One would have said that he lived only for that. His eyes never left me. He watched me as one watches an enemy. I was happy! (*a pause*) And when I told him that I loved him, when he learned that it was true, he seemed suddenly so . . . so happy, too . . . so relieved. I thought that I had really won him. (*a pause*) He was like a child. He closed his eyes, and let himself sink into my arms, as if he placed everything in my hands. On his lips he had a sweet, mysterious smile. Then, a long while later, a very long while later, he opened his eyes again and said to me almost laughing: "How we are going to suffer, Isabella!" I felt suddenly very cold . . .

LA MOTA. I understand, Signora . . . But you may be sure that he will return once more, dirtier perhaps, and more bitter . . . But he will return. What other than that might you fear? . . .

ISABELLA. I fear that he may fall in love for the first time.

LA MOTA. But that is madness . . . You know very well . . .

Don Juan enters on these words.

Scene II

DON JUAN. Madness? . . . Madness is the loveliest word I know. May I inquire where the madness is, and what it is? Good day, La Mota. Good day, Isabella.

ISABELLA. Good day, Juan. I was saying to Don Manuel La Mota that for several days you haven't seemed well. You are different . . . You aren't as lighthearted . . . At night, your sleep is so troubled. When I watch you sleep . . .

DON JUAN. I think I told you, Isabella, that I don't like people to watch me sleep. Besides, I'm sorry to contradict you, but I feel very lighthearted indeed. And what has madness to do with all this?

LA MOTA. I feel that it was madness . . .

DON JUAN. You are completely right, my good fellow. Isabella is mad . . .

LA MOTA. Perhaps you are slightly responsible. I must leave now. Excuse me, Signora . . . (*He leaves*)

Scene III

ISABELLA. Did you have a good journey, darling?

DON JUAN. No. I wore out two horses . . . Córdoba is far away.

ISABELLA. You arrived this morning in Seville?

DON JUAN. No. Yesterday.

ISABELLA. Oh! . . . (*a pause*) I was hoping . . .

DON JUAN. You were hoping? . . .

ISABELLA. To see you a bit sooner. We've been apart for five days.

DON JUAN. It's as long as that?

ISABELLA. That isn't long. One doesn't count the time when one is dead. I have been dead during your absence.

DON JUAN. How happy one must be to love in that way . . .

ISABELLA. Yes, Juan. It is awful and magnificent. If happiness means knowing no rest, struggling incessantly with a thousand invisible and imaginary enemies, dreaming of what one cannot have, wanting what is refused one . . . If happiness means to have the soul of the rich and the clothing of the poor, then I am happy.

A long pause.

DON JUAN. I am going to ask you something, Isabella.

ISABELLA. I am ready, Juan.

DON JUAN. You grant me my request in advance?

ISABELLA. Yes, Juan.

DON JUAN. Take care. You don't know what I am going to ask.

ISABELLA. I told you once, Juan, that I loved you for better or for worse.

DON JUAN. I know, Isabella. That is why I am going to ask you something difficult.

ISABELLA. I am ready.

DON JUAN. Do you know Anne de Ulloa?

Isabella draws back.

ISABELLA. (*in a whisper*) Yes.

DON JUAN. Are you already afraid?

ISABELLA. A little, Juan. What are you going to tell me?

DON JUAN. I think that I may be in love with her.

ISABELLA. No!

DON JUAN. (*gently*) I have not finished, Isabella.

ISABELLA. You know that La Mota, your friend, your only friend, lives only for the day when he can marry her. He told me that he was going to ask for her hand. You can't do that, Juan! You can't do that to your friend.

DON JUAN. I know, Isabella. But if I were to love her, it would be something so great that friendship itself could not survive it . . . And I haven't yet finished.

ISABELLA. What more is there to say?

DON JUAN. I don't know her. I have never spoken to her. She is still so young she only goes out accompanied by her father or her nurse. I must meet her alone.

ISABELLA. And you are counting on me to . . .

DON JUAN. (*gently, pitilessly*) Yes, Isabella.

ISABELLA. Juan, Juan, of all the women in Seville, you choose me to present you your future mistress?

DON JUAN. You promised.

ISABELLA. Not that. Then you have no heart whatever?

DON JUAN. You promised. No matter what. You promised in advance.

ISABELLA. No, I won't. You don't realize how cruel you are? You don't realize how you are tearing me apart? You tell me in two sentences that I have ceased to exist for you, and that you love someone else. Juan! And you would like me to receive her here in my house, and give you my bedroom, too, I suppose?

DON JUAN. I did not say that you had ceased to exist for me. I have a great deal of affection for you, Isabella. But this is so completely different. She is perhaps the whole world to me.

ISABELLA. (*to herself*) I knew this would happen.

DON JUAN. Besides, it is too late. She is coming.

ISABELLA. You dared? . . .

DON JUAN. I dared. Counting on your favorable reply, I took the liberty of sending her a little note this morning, signed by you, in which you ask her to do you the favor of coming to see you this afternoon. She will be here shortly . . .

ISABELLA. She will not cross this threshold.

DON JUAN. I fear you're making a mistake, Isabella.

ISABELLA. I swear to you that she will not cross this threshold.

DON JUAN. Don't swear, Isabella. She will cross it. And you will receive her very agreeably. After the three of us talk for a few minutes, you will do me the favor of going into the park to see if the gardeners have clipped your hedges as you ordered. You need have no fear. I shall behave very correctly.

ISABELLA. It's useless, Juan. I won't do that.

DON JUAN. Why insist that you won't, my dear? You will.

ISABELLA. No.

DON JUAN. Yes, Isabella. Don't force me to continue a conversation that I dislike as much as you do. I know that you will. For several reasons! The first is wholly practical: your opposition will not prevent anything. If I don't see her here, I shall see her elsewhere; and you will lose the benefit of my gesture.

ISABELLA. You are vile!

DON JUAN. The second reason will impress you more than the first. If you do not receive Anne de Ulloa under the terms that I have indicated to you, you will not see me again as long as you live.
Enter Pepita.

PEPITA. Señorita Anne de Ulloa has just come, Señora. She says that you are awaiting her.

99

A long pause.

DON JUAN. I'm also waiting, Isabella.

ISABELLA. (*softly and harshly*) I hate you, Juan. (*louder*) Tell the Señorita that I shall receive her.

DON JUAN. (*to Pepita*) Show her in. (*to Isabella*) Remember, Isabella. And take care.

Pepita shows Anne in.

Scene IV

ANNE. Thank you so much for your kind invitation, Señora.

A pause.

ISABELLA. It is a pleasure to see you, Señorita. May I present my friend, Don Juan Tenorio.

ANNE. Don Manuel La Mota has often spoken of you.

DON JUAN. I am delighted to meet you, Señorita.

A pause. Isabella gestures to them to sit down.

ISABELLA. Manuel La Mota is a very fine man. He is honest and good. You feel very close to him, don't you, Juan?

DON JUAN. (*distractedly, his gaze fixed on Anne*) Yes, very.

ANNE. I like him very much, too.

ISABELLA. He has a kind of veneration for you, Señorita. I think there is nothing that he would not do to please you. The other evening, seeing us so happy together, Juan and me, he told us . . .

DON JUAN. (*interrupting Isabella*) Yes, he spoke to us with such affection of you and your father. They are almost the same age, I believe . . .

ANNE. Yes. It is rare for an uncle and a nephew to be the same age.

DON JUAN. So that you seem to find a second father in your cousin . . .

ANNE. He is very good to me.

A pause. Don Juan looks purposefully at Isabella.

ISABELLA. (*with some effort*) Excuse me for a moment. I must speak to the gardener . . .

Don Juan walks quickly toward her, and under the pretext of kissing her hand, leads her gently to the door.

Scene V

ANNE. (*softly*) Why did you ask her to leave us alone together?

DON JUAN. (*smiling*) I asked her that, Señorita?

ANNE. Yes, Don Juan; you are cruel.

DON JUAN. Less cruel than you are intelligent.

ANNE. I am not intelligent. I have a feeling for things. When I entered this room a few moments ago, I was warned of danger. I had not yet noticed you. Danger took on at once the outlines of your face.

DON JUAN. (*bowing*) You do me a great honor, Señorita.

ANNE. Don't be foolish. So, this is Don Juan Tenorio. How strange it is!

DON JUAN. And what, may I ask, is so strange?

ANNE. This meeting. I was thinking of you on my way here. I've been wanting to meet you for a long time . . . Your . . . renown has even reached me. But you don't seem so frightening in the flesh.

DON JUAN. Don't I, Anne?

ANNE. One must just be able to read what goes on within you.

DON JUAN. That's all, Anne, and that is not so difficult.

ANNE. No. Not as difficult as you would like to think. (*a pause*) You have not yet told me why you asked the Duchess to leave us alone.

DON JUAN. Read that within me. It is surely less difficult than I should like it to be.

ANNE. I'd like to hear it from you.

DON JUAN. Well, Anne, simply because I had no other way of seeing you alone. I saw you a few days ago in the cathedral. I had a strange feeling then deep inside me. I had the impression that there was a link between us and that you had something to teach me. Is it true?

ANNE. Perhaps.

DON JUAN. It came from you like a call. And it did not resemble desire. It was new and strong, like the wind on the sea. I wanted to

101

go to you. But your father and my friend La Mota were watching over you closely.

ANNE. Your friend, La Mota? Do you have friends, Don Juan?

DON JUAN. He's the only one.

ANNE. But without the slightest scruple you would seduce the girl he loves and wants to marry.

DON JUAN. "Without scruple" is inexact! I would have some scruples about it. And besides, since you don't love him, he has no claim over you.

ANNE. Who told you that I did not love him?

DON JUAN. No one. But I know it.

ANNE. You are sure of yourself, Don Juan!

DON JUAN. I also sense things, Anne.

A pause.

ANNE. And you, Don Juan, have you ever loved anyone?

DON JUAN. No, Anne.

ANNE. And you are happy?

DON JUAN. No, Anne. Because I have no other reason to live.

ANNE. What do you expect of this love?

DON JUAN. Freedom.

ANNE. Go on.

DON JUAN. There is nothing more to say. Freedom. Love should give it.

A pause.

ANNE. What freedom?

DON JUAN. The freedom of the fowler who is tired of watching a bird beat against its cage, and who one day opens the door of the cage. The bird is free, and he at the same time is freed of his cage.

ANNE. The comparison is ingenious, Don Juan. But, for the moment, you would like to put me in your cage.

DON JUAN. (*gravely*) No, Anne.

ANNE. Take care. I am not a canary that is to be locked up. I have my sky and my wings. And if I sing, I'll sing outside.

DON JUAN. (*in the same tone of voice*) I hope so with all my heart.

ANNE. (*her eyes fixed on those of Don Juan*) So be it.

A pause.

102

DON JUAN. You have a beautiful face.

ANNE. Like those of all the women you have betrayed. Do you see them again at times in your dreams?

DON JUAN. Often.

ANNE. That must be frightful!

DON JUAN. In the long run, yes . . . (*smiling*) One must think of one's salvation.

ANNE. You are still far from that. (*a pause*) Will you keep in your gallery the face of the Duchess when she left this room?

DON JUAN. I prefer to have only pleasant memories. All the faces in my dreams are happy ones.

A pause.

ANNE. It is easy to be cruel toward people who love you, Don Juan. She loves you. I suppose that you would be astonished if one were to call your attitude something other than cruelty; cowardice, for example. One can put up, if need be, with cruelty. But in a noble-man cowardice is indeed serious. (*a pause*) It is curious. You are the embodiment of all the defects, all the vices that I despise most in this world, a single one of which would suffice to remove me from someone forever. And yet I find you most attractive. (*a short pause*) You are pure. I shall pray for you.

DON JUAN. (*bowing, half gravely, half jocundly*) Thank you, Anne.

ANNE. If I were wise, I'd accept La Mota immediately. He has all the qualities I admire — honesty, modesty, kindness. All that you lack, Don Juan. And he loves me.

DON JUAN. I'm astonished that you hesitate for a second.

ANNE. I like risks; with him there is none. And his soul has no need of my help.

DON JUAN. Those are noble reasons. Will you add to them that you do not feel the slightest love for him?

ANNE. I do not love you either. At least, not in the way you want. My life is still ahead of me. I'm very young, Don Juan. It was not long ago that I put aside my toys and my dolls.

DON JUAN. (*bending closely over her*) Did you take them to bed with you at night?

103

ANNE. (*recoiling brusquely*) Why do you try to unnerve me? I thought you more adroit. That is not the way to win me.

DON JUAN. Forgive me. That was rather poor, I must say. I want only what you want, Anne.

ANNE. We'll see.

DON JUAN. What do you do now that you have given up playing with dolls?

ANNE. I dream.

DON JUAN. May I ask the subject of your dreams?

ANNE. I dream of a difficult life. One day I am a saint. Another, I am the lowest servant in my palace. One day, I free cities by speaking of God to my soldiers. On another, I care for lepers or wash the feet of the poor.

DON JUAN. (*ironically*) All that stretched out on the cushions of your bed?

ANNE. Yes, all that stretched out on the cushions of my bed. But the dream will one day become reality. I have already dreamed that I would devote myself to you, Don Juan.

DON JUAN. Do tell me about that. My future interests me enormously.

ANNE. I tell them badly. And then they are dreams. Let us rather speak of you. What sort of little boy were you?

DON JUAN. I was impossible — proud, weak, a bully. And I had a horror of little girls.

ANNE. You have changed!

DON JUAN. They frightened me. I didn't know what to say to them. And you couldn't hit them.

ANNE. I liked boys very much. And I didn't hesitate to hit them.

DON JUAN. We might have fought . . .

ANNE. No doubt. Who would have won?

A pause.

DON JUAN. You are so delightfully fresh, Anne. I should have met you as you are now when I was fifteen years younger.

ANNE. You would not even have looked at me.

DON JUAN. You are right. I may have to be all that I am to understand all that you are . . .

ANNE. Just as I may have to know nothing of all I know nothing of in order to hope for what I hope . . .

DON JUAN. (*after a pause*) You are childhood personified, Anne, and you bring mine back to me. With those lovely little hands of yours.

He takes her hands. She draws them back immediately.

ANNE. No, Don Juan. Don't fall back on easy compliments and expected gestures.

DON JUAN. I am sincere, Anne.

ANNE. Your tone, your speech are not. Don't be someone else all the time. One would think that you were replying to yourself.

DON JUAN. I am the man you wish me to be.

ANNE. Good. You are going to prove it to me by returning to Isabella.

DON JUAN. But . . .

ANNE. Do not interrupt me. Neither of us is ready for what you wish, Don Juan. And nothing could grow up between us now except bewilderment and destruction. Go back to Isabella. Ask her to forgive you for the way you acted just now. (*a pause*) And don't expect anything of me!

DON JUAN. I do not love her.

ANNE. You should not have taken her then. And, furthermore, you don't love me either. The sacrifice is not great then. (*a pause*) Beings are not things, Don Juan. They are not birds, either, as in your fable. They are men and women like us, as worthy as you and I of living, of loving, and of being happy. That you must learn.

DON JUAN. (*with amused resignation*) Yes, Anne. What have I still to learn?

ANNE. Not to make fun of me. I don't like that at all. (*a pause*) One day perhaps, when you are worthy of it, I shall tell you that you have lovely eyes. And I shall allow you to kiss me.

DON JUAN. Will that be a long time from now?

ANNE. That will depend on you. (*a pause*) I will save you, Don Juan. (*a pause*) I know that my task will be great. But that is the kind of affection I feel for you.

A long pause.

DON JUAN. Are you an angel?

ANNE. No, a virgin.

Isabella comes in.

Scene VI

ISABELLA. I've taken far too long. Forgive me . . .

DON JUAN. We spoke of very interesting things while we were waiting.

ISABELLA. I don't doubt it. Love, I suppose, was the chief concern of this . . . exchange of views.

ANNE. Yes. Don Juan told me what he felt for you.

ISABELLA. He . . . He told you of this love? . . .

ANNE. (*her eyes on those of Don Juan*) Didn't you, Don Juan? This freedom, this freshness . . .

ISABELLA. That's what you said, Juan?

DON JUAN. (*as if suddenly aware of Isabella*) No . . .

ANNE. (*vivaciously*) That is what he thought . . .

ISABELLA. Did you think it, Juan?

DON JUAN. I thought that there comes a time in the life of every man when a certain choice is open to him.

ANNE. And you have chosen, Don Juan?

DON JUAN. I have chosen, Anne.

ANNE. Take care! This choice is final. For this time will not come round again.

DON JUAN. I know . . . It is the last chance that I have given myself.

ANNE. . . . that has been given you.

DON JUAN. If you prefer.

ISABELLA. I don't understand any part of this . . . Juan, Juan, is it true that you love me?

A long pause.

ANNE. I must be going . . . People are expecting me. Don't bother; I can find my way.

Don Juan leads her to the door and returns to Isabella.

106

Scene VII

ISABELLA. Juan, answer me. Are you joking again? Or is it true that you love me? (*Don Juan remains silent*) I implore you. I can't bear your silence.

Don Juan draws away from her and turns around.

DON JUAN. Don't believe her, Isabella.

ISABELLA. What do you mean?

DON JUAN. I don't love you.

ISABELLA. But all that you have just . . .

DON JUAN. (*interrupting her*) All that was true. But it wasn't said about you.

ISABELLA. About her? And she dared play this hateful trick on me!

DON JUAN. It was not a trick, Isabella. She wanted to bring us together. She saw that I had forced you to receive her. She wanted to pay for the suffering she had caused you by bringing you a greater joy. She is generous!

ISABELLA. She is, indeed.

DON JUAN. She is one of those persons who model reality on their dreams and are right even when the evidence is against them. She does not love me, you may be sure. If she did, would she have done that? But she wants to "save" me, as she puts it.

ISABELLA. . . . by dragging you into her nets!

DON JUAN. You are becoming vulgar, Isabella. She is pure.

ISABELLA. She is dangerous. To send you back to me is very clever! Some fine gestures are worth the trouble! She does not for a moment doubt that my cause is lost.

DON JUAN. She did not play such a game. I will not allow you to attack her unjustly.

ISABELLA. You see that she has got what she wanted.

DON JUAN. I have never felt what I feel now.

ISABELLA. You say that every time, Juan.

DON JUAN. No, Isabella, you do not understand. For the first time, I have been reduced to something other than myself. I no longer lead, I am led.

107

ISABELLA. You will have her like the others, and that will be the end of it.

DON JUAN. She is a virgin.

ISABELLA. She will not be the first!

DON JUAN. This is different. I would have deceived the others by not having them. With her it would be the contrary. It would be stupid to end up like that: it would mean killing something that is beginning and that will perhaps be beautiful.

ISABELLA. She is a doll like the others who will say "yes" when you lay her on her back.

DON JUAN. I'm going to astonish you, Isabella. But I swear to you that I have no desire to lay her on her back, as you put it. If I do one day other than in marriage, it will be the greatest, the only failure in my life.

ISABELLA. Other than in marriage. You are at that point, Juan?

DON JUAN. She is the future of love, Isabella.

ISABELLA. And I am not even the past of love. I am Isabella who has always wept. (*a pause*) But I also have something to tell you, Juan. (*a pause*) I am leaving you.

DON JUAN. You are leaving me?

ISABELLA. Yes. I can't go on, Juan. I am broken. I've endured so much, wept so much that I have the feeling you could finish me off right now with a flick of your little finger. I want to try to live again.

DON JUAN. I understand, Isabella. What are you going to do?

A pause.

ISABELLA. I am going to get married, too.

A pause.

DON JUAN. That is quite unexpected. May I know? . . .

ISABELLA. What good would it do to tell you his name? Is that important?

DON JUAN. Important to me!

ISABELLA. No, I don't want another duel. You will learn it only when I have left Seville with him. All you need know is that he loves me and wants to marry me. He is pressing me for an answer. I have always rejected him. But just now, while you were with this girl, I decided to accept him.

DON JUAN. Has he already taken you to bed?

ISABELLA. (*pretending to hesitate*) What difference can that make to you since I am no longer anything to you?

DON JUAN. Answer me. Has he taken you to bed?

ISABELLA. But I don't understand your insistence, Juan. You tell me that you are in love with this girl. You have given me clearly to understand that I had nothing more to hope from you in the future. What difference can my actions make to you? From now on, they concern me alone.

DON JUAN. Will you please answer when I ask you a question. Has he taken you to bed?

ISABELLA. He tried.

DON JUAN. And? . . .

ISABELLA. I did not want to.

DON JUAN. You are in love with him?

ISABELLA. It is not my habit to have feelings that I can substitute for others.

DON JUAN. Then why are you marrying him?

ISABELLA. Because I want to try finally to be happy.

DON JUAN. You hope to be happy with someone you don't love? Learn from my experience. It is difficult.

ISABELLA. Perhaps not happy, but in peace. To live in peace, Juan. To forget that charm with which you hold me captive, to escape from this circle in which I struggle like an animal caught in a net. To be free! Free! To be able to wake up in the morning without feeling, even before I open my eyes, this burning cancer in my breast. To look at the sky, to taste the wind, touch the trunk of a tree, the water of a spring, and to know that I'm still alive. To go to sleep at night saying to myself: "Tomorrow will be another day. And a peaceful one . . ."

DON JUAN. There is no peace in this world for beings without love. Death is preferable!

ISABELLA. I shall think about it, Juan, if I fail.

A pause.

109

DON JUAN. Do not do that, Isabella.

ISABELLA. It is too late, Juan. I have written to say I would leave with him.

DON JUAN. (*violently*) Where is that letter?

ISABELLA. The maid is taking it to him.

Don Juan runs toward the door, opens it, and calls out.

DON JUAN. Pepita. (*Seconds later, Pepita appears*) Did the Señora give you a letter just now?

PEPITA. Yes, Señor.

DON JUAN. Have you already delivered it?

PEPITA. Not yet, Señor.

DON JUAN. Give it to me! (*Pepita hesitates, looks at Isabella, who is motionless and silent, and finally draws a letter from her bodice and gives it to Don Juan*) Good. (*Pepita leaves. Don Juan unfolds the letter, reads it quickly, then tears it up*)

ISABELLA. (*hiding her happiness*) I no longer recognize you, Juan. You are behaving like a husband all of a sudden.

DON JUAN. Don't joke, Isabella. You have hurt me.

ISABELLA. And you think I have not been hurt. What I have suffered is completely natural? That's all over, Juan. I'm leaving. You were a God to me, but the gods themselves sometimes tire the patience of their followers. (*She pretends to start to leave*)

DON JUAN. Wait, Isabella. Wait. The god gives in. I love you.

A long pause.

ISABELLA. What did you say, Juan?

DON JUAN. (*slowly*) I love you, Isabella.

A long pause.

ISABELLA. You love me! (*a pause*) No, it's not possible! You are still lying!

DON JUAN. Isabella, how could I express it to you in any other way? I love you. I love you. Just now when you told me you were going away with that man, when I read that letter, when you told me that he had already tried to seduce you, I felt suddenly how drawn I am to you. I have gradually taken the habit of considering you my property. Forgive me. It's as if I had been robbed during my sleep. It's very curious and very disagreeable.

110

ISABELLA. You love me, Juan? Say it again so that I may be sure to hear it!

DON JUAN. I love you, Isabella.

A pause.

ISABELLA. This is the moment I've been waiting for for so long, the moment for which I've lived ever since I've known you. You love me, Don Juan. You, the miser who has suddenly become prodigal. The difficulty is that you have already lied to me so often, Juan. You have accustomed me to never being sure of my unhappiness nor of my happiness. I don't dare believe anything any more. You change so often.

DON JUAN. Isabella, do you think that I could pretend at a time like this? Look at me, look in my eyes. Do they seem to lie? They are lost in yours. I love you, Isabella.

ISABELLA. A few moments ago, you spoke to me of this girl in the same tone of voice, Juan. She was the angel who had beckoned to you. She was . . . heaven knows what. The key, the clue! She was the future of love, of your life, your dreams. And I was the sad Isabella, whom you hated right down to her tears.

DON JUAN. That is true. Together we have tracked down an old ghost. But you are my living soul, Isabella. The rest is but the pursuit of the wind.

ISABELLA. My dearest, why have you made me suffer so much?

DON JUAN. Because I suffered so myself. Because I envied your certainty, I was sure of nothing. Because my only assurance was the love of others. It is fitting that now I am unloved.

ISABELLA. Unloved! . . . Oh, Juan, have you forgotten everything then? Have you forgotten Octavio? My fiancé, to whom I had promised my hand — and you know what a promise meant to me. You killed him, he is dead because of me. And I was happy to see you come back untouched. Have you forgotten all that I left behind in Naples, my country that I've left without a thought, my honor, to which I was more attached than my life . . . I would have renounced God himself if you had asked me, for you were my God on earth. Have you forgotten everything, my dearest? Have you forgotten that night in Granada, when you forced me,

111

right in front of the servant girl at the inn, to make the bed that you were going to occupy with her? And I did it because I loved you. Have you forgotten the day when you beat me as one would not beat even a slave because I dared to think other than you about heaven knows what? And I said nothing because I loved you. Do you think that has cost me nothing? Oh, Juan, have you forgotten who I was before I knew you: my self-respect, my virtue, my pride . . . All that I have given you along with myself. For you I have taken vows, Juan. I have entered that sulfurous cell where all those who serve you lie moaning. How I have wept!

DON JUAN. Forgive me, Isabella. Now I give you one moment that will perhaps pay for all that . . . I, Don Juan, here I am before you, and it is my turn to beg. And I kneel at your feet. (*He kneels before her*) And I say to you: "I love you, Isabella, as you loved me."

ISABELLA. Yes, Juan, I am paid back for everything.

DON JUAN. It is the first time in my life that I have uttered those words. They have a strange and sad flavor on my lips, like that of accepted defeat. You win, Isabella. And it is my turn to lose you.

ISABELLA. One does not lose what one has gained forever, Juan. I have often prayed that my love be torn from my heart. But my heart would have to be torn out with it. My dearest, if I loved you less, I might savor this moment when, for the first time, you have given yourself wholly to me. I might avenge myself for all that I have suffered, and dispose of you in my fashion, just as you have always disposed of me. But I would not know how to do so. (*a pause*) And at this time, I make you the supreme sacrifice of not lying to you. I love you, Juan. I have never loved anyone but you, I shall never love anyone but you. Today and forever, now and in eternity.

Don Juan gets up slowly. A subtle change starts to take place gradually in him, leading up to the desperate violence with which the act closes.

DON JUAN. And that letter? . . .

ISABELLA. I deceived you just now. I had begun that letter in a moment of despair. I finished it so you might read it. But I would never have sent it. I wanted to know if you were still capable of jealousy.

DON JUAN. Now you know. Are you happy?

ISABELLA. Yes, Juan. As happy as can be . . .

DON JUAN. It is your victory.

ISABELLA. My victory? Does one employ for love the language of war? Let come what may, Juan. I put my blind arms around you. Tonight for the first time you will cry out upon my body . . .

DON JUAN. (*mechanically*) I shall cry out . . .

ISABELLA. All our nights together I have waited for the cry that would come from the depths of your being to tell me that you loved me. I howled like an animal. I endured each time that new, terrible thing engendered by my love. And I saw far off, as at sea, your concentrated face closing quietly upon its pleasure. I moved out toward you. I signaled desperately to you with all my being. But we never reached the same shore.

DON JUAN. (*after a long pause*) I shall never forget that you have betrayed me, Isabella.

ISABELLA. (*All the replies that follow come very quickly*) But I did not betray you, Juan. It's just a little trick I played on you . . .

DON JUAN. It was betrayal.

ISABELLA. I have never been anything but yours, all yours.

DON JUAN You have tried to flee from me, and you have succeeded.

ISABELLA. No, it is not true.

DON JUAN. You should not have lied.

ISABELLA. I did it to get you back.

DON JUAN. It is by lying to me that you lost me. You do not love me.

ISABELLA. Oh, Juan, what must I do then? Must I tear out my tongue and cut off my hands to prove that I love you?

DON JUAN. You should not have cheated. A trickster is not a lover. A lover suffers and keeps quiet.

ISABELLA. I love you, Juan, as no woman has ever loved a man. I love you like God.

DON JUAN. One gives oneself up to God without reservation and without hope, without asking anything and without expecting anything.

ISABELLA. That's how I am yours, Juan. If I had done for my God a quarter of what I have done for my love, what a great saint I would be today. (*a long pause*) What can I still give that I have not given?

A pause. Don Juan draws a thin dagger from his doublet and extends it casually to Isabella.

DON JUAN. Your life, for example.

ISABELLA. You want it, Juan? (*A long pause. She extends her hand slowly toward the dagger*)

DON JUAN. (*drawing the dagger quickly back toward him*) No, that would be too easy.

ISABELLA. Then, what do you want of me?

DON JUAN. I want you to go kill that man.

Isabella recoils in terror.

ISABELLA. You are mad, Juan. What has he done to you?

DON JUAN. That is not the question. If he had *done* something to me, as you put it, I would kill him quite easily myself. I simply want to know how far you will push the love you have for me and the disdain you have for him.

ISABELLA. I swear to you, Juan, on your very self, you alone exist for me.

DON JUAN. I know, Isabella. (*a pause*) One more reason for carrying out what I have proposed. If you feel indifferent toward him
. . .

ISABELLA. Indifference does not lead to crime.

DON JUAN. Love can sometimes lead to it. The love you have for me will lead you to it.

ISABELLA. No, Juan. No, it is useless. Not that. Not that.

DON JUAN. You will do it, Isabella.

ISABELLA. No, Juan. I cannot. I will not.

DON JUAN. You will, Isabella.

ISABELLA. No, it's impossible. Not I. Not I. Ask me no matter what else. No matter what. Not that.

DON JUAN. Unfortunately that happens to be the only thing I want to see you do.

ISABELLA. Ah, why was I ever born? Dear God!

114

DON JUAN. I am waiting, Isabella.

She extends her arm to seize the dagger, then recoils again.

ISABELLA. Not that, Juan. Not that! . . .

DON JUAN. Isabella, for the last time! . . .

ISABELLA. Juan, Juan, where will you lead me?

DON JUAN. To the peaks that you wanted to reach, Isabella. You are very fortunate to know that altitude. (*He hands her the dagger again*) I offer you the opportunity to love. (*Isabella takes the dagger, looks at it a moment, looks at Don Juan who is still expressionless, and wants to use it upon herself. But Don Juan, quicker than she, seizes her wrist*) Would you be a coward, Isabella? Why want to leave me so soon?

ISABELLA. I am at the end of my strength . . .

DON JUAN. I should have thought that passion sustained its elect better than that. Can one experience at the same time ecstasies as divine and weaknesses as human? (*a pause*) Well, Isabella, I am still waiting. (*A pause. He releases Isabella's wrist*)

ISABELLA. Oh, God, who gazes down upon me now, take into account all my suffering on the day you judge me! (*She goes slowly toward the door*)

DON JUAN. Where are you going, Isabella? (*She looks at him for a moment without seeming to hear him*) Where are you going?

ISABELLA. I am going where you ordered me to go.

DON JUAN. (*bursting out laughing*) So, you believed it? . . . You really believed that I would let you kill that man?

A pause. Isabella looks at him without seeming to understand.

ISABELLA. What do you mean?

DON JUAN. So, you took this little scene seriously. You believed it . . . Ah, how amusing! . . .

ISABELLA. What do you mean, Juan?

DON JUAN. But it was a joke, of course. I am not an assassin.

ISABELLA. What do you mean, Juan? (*She lets the dagger fall to the floor, staggers forward, bursts into hysterical laughter, turns around and falls to the floor laughing and crying at the same time*)

115

DON JUAN. (*on the point of leaving*) Farewell, my dear! You can see for yourself the dangers of lying.

ISABELLA. (*between her sobs*) Juan, when will you stop torturing me?

DON JUAN. Probably never . . . That is the only way I can be faithful.

He leaves. The intermittent sobbing of Isabella, still on the floor, may be heard for a moment longer. Then

CURTAIN

Act III

The scene represents Anne de Ulloa's apartment, in the palace of her father, the Commander of Seville. On the court side, windows opening on the palace park. On the garden side, windows opening on the street. Upstage, two doors: one opening on a palace corridor, the other leading to Anne's bedroom. A corner of the room is given over to the oratory (a large crucifix, a prayer stool). Furniture of the period, tables, chairs, armchairs, cushions. Candelabra, a brass lamp on a console table. It is morning. As the curtain rises, Anne, seated, is working on a tapestry. Mamita, the nurse, returning from the city, enters. She embraces Anne.

Scene I

MAMITA. Good morning, my sweet. Good morning, darling. Did you sleep well?

ANNE. (*continuing her work*) Yes, Mamita. Thank you.

MAMITA. You look so pale. Why don't we go out for a while together? There's a lovely breeze. Your rosy cheeks will fade away if you stay locked up in this room like a nun in a convent. And that hussy Belisa never opens the windows! . . . (*She opens the windows*)

ANNE. (*a little impatiently*) Please stop it, Mamita!

MAMITA. What is the matter with you, darling? You've been a different person for some time. Are you ill?

ANNE. (*still impatient*) No, Mamita, I'm very well.

MAMITA. If you have any trouble, angel, you must tell me. You know that I have no other concern on earth but you.

ANNE. (*still impatient*) Yes, Mamita, I know. But I'm very well, I assure you. (*a short pause*) What's the news from town this morning?

MAMITA. (*reciting very quickly*) Two galleons arrived from India last night. They are said to hold enormous riches. I saw one of the crew; he was speaking to a gathering on the cathedral square. He was saying that the men and women over there go around completely naked, and paint their bodies red and white. They have hair as thick as horses' tails, and behind hangs a long strip they never cut. They don't have weapons like ours, but only pointed sticks to which they attach shark's teeth. They worship alien gods and build temples to them all of gold. Doña Francisca de Guadarra's dog died of fever. She's made herself sick grieving over it. I met the doctor on the way to her house. (*without a break*) Don Juan Tenorio is going to leave Seville. The King is sending him to Sicily. (*Anne's needle remains poised above her tapestry*) What else did I hear? Ah, yes, there will be day after tomorrow a great auto-da-fé in front of the cathedral; seven heretics will be burned at stake. I believe that's all.

A long pause.

ANNE. Is he leaving alone?

MAMITA. Who?

ANNE. Don Juan.

MAMITA. I don't know who's going with him.

ANNE. Is his Italian mistress leaving, too?

MAMITA. I don't know. (*a short pause. She continues*) It seems to me that you are speaking of things that a well-brought-up young lady should not know about, my dearest. What is certain is that he is leaving. And that's fine, as far as I'm concerned. He's a man it would be better for you not to know, my sweet. He came last month to visit your father much more often than simple politeness required.

ANNE. Don't be silly, Mamita.

MAMITA. Do you think I'm blind? And it happened too often for

118

your peace of mind and mine that chance brought you face to face in a hallway or garden. You were seen much too long with him at the party your father gave last week. Respectable young ladies should avoid him like the plague. I am happy he's leaving. I detest that man. He's like a vulture.

ANNE. An eagle, Mamita. And I am not happy that he's leaving.

A pause. She sits up suddenly very straight in her armchair, then bursts into sobs. Mamita hurries to her.

MAMITA. What is the matter, Anne? God in heaven, you're in love with that man. (*Anne sobs without answering*) My little darling, if you'd had the good luck to break both your legs the day you met him, you'd have been better off.

ANNE. It's not what you think, Mamita! He needs me.

MAMITA. He told you that?

ANNE. No, I told him. But he knows. I want to save him.

MAMITA. My poor darling, he has bewitched you, too. May the Lord protect you! It is you who must be saved, if it is not too late already.

ANNE. He needs me.

MAMITA. He needs one victim more. And he has found the tenderest and the purest, my lamb, my lily, my angel, my darling doe! Ah, he will be damned for ten eternities.

ANNE. He has not laid a hand on me, Mamita. He loves me. He will perhaps marry me.

MAMITA. Him? A thousand and one girls have believed that before you, and what they have given him, their tears will not buy back!

ANNE. You don't understand, Mamita. I am what he has always sought, what he needs in order to live. He loves me.

MAMITA. If he loved you, he would not leave.

ANNE. It is an order from the King. (*a short pause*) And he has not yet left.

Enter Belisa.

BELISA. Don Juan Tenorio would be pleased if you would consent to receive him, Señorita.

ANNE. (*to Mamita*) You see! (*to Belisa*) Show him in at once! (*to Mamita*) Leave us alone, Mamita.

MAMITA. But . . .

ANNE. (*imperiously*) Leave us, I say.

Mamita hesitates, then leaves as Anne gestures to her. Don Juan enters.

Scene II

DON JUAN. Good day, Anne.

ANNE. Good day, Don Juan.

DON JUAN. I have sad news to bring you.

ANNE. I think I know what it is already. You are leaving Seville?

DON JUAN. Yes, I should leave Seville. But . . .

ANNE. But? . . .

DON JUAN. But I love you, Anne.

ANNE. No, not yet! You don't yet love me, and you must leave. (*a pause*) You will return? . . .

DON JUAN. Yes, Anne.

ANNE. Your path is filled with danger, Don Juan. You will meet many faces.

DON JUAN. Yours will not leave me.

ANNE. You will meet new women who have pleasing charms and secrets I don't know.

DON JUAN. I know them.

ANNE. Will you resist them?

DON JUAN. I will exorcise them by thinking of yours.

ANNE. I have only my faith to sustain me, Juan.

DON JUAN. You have the certainty of your purity. I shall have the certainty of my love.

ANNE. It's too soon to say so. You must struggle still against so many enemies yet alive in you.

DON JUAN. They have ceased resisting you, Anne. Have I not for two weeks proved that you alone count for me?

ANNE. Do you think that two weeks' devotion is enough to convince me of an undying love? I'm not accustomed to your way of measuring, Don Juan.

DON JUAN. When will I succeed in moving you, Anne? You are all that exists within me. That proud little image has triumphed over

120

all my memories and all my doubts. Smile at me! (*She smiles*) I am going to leave carrying away this last vision of you: a room open on the March sunlight, the curtains moving gently, that brass lamp lit by a ray of the sun . . . And you sitting there like a good little schoolgirl, her hands on that uncompleted work. And that smile on the hard little mouth I have never kissed . . . I shall remember the slope of your shoulder, the ripples in the silk over your bodice . . . That rose between your breasts . . . Its memory will make me feel less lonely. And when I am far away, I shall say: at that time, I was near her . . . A few steps from her . . . I shall be able to dream that I drew near you. (*He draws near her*) That I drew near you, touched you. (*He touches her forehead slightly at the hairline*) That I bent over you. (*He bends over her very slowly*) That I gazed at length into your eyes at my own image reflected upside down. (*He bends toward her mouth*) And you will say . . .

ANNE. (*crying*) No, Juan! . . .

DON JUAN. You will say: "No, Juan" in that voice. Exactly in that voice. And my dream will be over. Give me that rose. All must not be lost.

ANNE. (*in a slightly trembling voice*) Can it be that Don Juan as he grows old has begun collecting locks of hair and pressed flowers?

DON JUAN. "Your irony is impure, Don Juan; it is the weapon of the Devil!" Isn't that what you said once, Anne? And now it's you who insist on being witty.

ANNE. (*smiling and holding the rose out to him*) I don't want to be witty, Juan. It's because I want to weep. I was afraid of you for a second. And now I'm happy.

DON JUAN. Weep, my darling. I love you. Don Juan is not really accustomed to collecting pressed flowers. Nor is he accustomed to being repulsed when he wants to embrace a woman. But that Don Juan is dead: all that is left is a man who will often kiss this rose during his lonely evenings because it has touched your skin. All that is left is a man who must accept the fact that you refused his lips. . . . And who is happy you did.

ANNE. There are joys one is not ready to give nor to receive, Juan. A day will come when I shall know by looking at your face that you are the man for whom I've been waiting. That day, I shall also be the woman for whom you are waiting. Let us keep ourselves for that day, Juan. Let us keep ourselves for the day you become my husband.

DON JUAN. Yes, Anne.

ANNE. It is not to you alone that I cried "No!" but more particularly to myself: there is also in me thirst and shame, Juan, weakness and desire. I am made of flesh and I often dream of your arms. But what would have happened if you had touched my lips? You would have reduced one more woman to your mercy. But what would you have dreamed of during your journey?

DON JUAN. I love you, Anne.

ANNE. Would you have seen again the schoolgirl sitting here, the rose, the curtains ruffling in the breeze, and the sunlight on the lamp?

DON JUAN. No, Anne. I would have forgotten all to remember a kiss.

ANNE. But not my kiss. Love is difficult and slow, Juan. One must live with it at length in the imagination in order to be able to experience it in reality one day.

DON JUAN. Yes, Anne. How do you know that?

ANNE. Because I love you.

A long pause.

DON JUAN. I am going to leave, Anne.

ANNE. (*in a different tone of voice*) Today?

DON JUAN. Tonight probably. Or at dawn.

ANNE. Isabella will accompany you?

DON JUAN. You know very well that she will not. Why do you speak to me of her?

ANNE. She will go on suffering . . .

DON JUAN. Do you see any way of avoiding it?

ANNE. No . . . I don't see any way now.

A pause.

DON JUAN. Farewell, Anne. The ship that will bear me away will have on its prow a face like yours, which will defy the waves, just as yours will defy distance.

ANNE. Farewell, Juan. It's strange to say so, but I have confidence in you. When will I see you again?

DON JUAN. If need be, I will command the winds and the tides. I will tell them that my love waits for me beyond the sea. And they will obey me, for neither God nor man could keep you from being soon again in my arms.

ANNE. Do not be blasphemous, Juan. The patience of God is perhaps not infinite. (*a pause*) Au revoir. Take care.

He gazes at her at length and starts to leave, as the Commander enters.

Scene III

THE COMMANDER. I thought you had left for Sicily.

DON JUAN. I expect to leave this evening, Señor. But I wanted before I left to say good-bye to Señorita de Ulloa.

THE COMMANDER. I presume that you are not unaware that it is improper for you to come into her private apartments without having asked my permission and without being accompanied by me?

ANNE. Father, please, when I heard Don Juan was leaving, I begged him to come.

THE COMMANDER. Are you mad, daughter? Have you been brought up like a wench in some inn? There are too many women whose names are associated with this man for me to entertain the idea that yours is to be added to them.

DON JUAN. It is rare that one can insult me with impunity, Señor! You are, I must say, the only man I've ever permitted to do so.

ANNE. Don Juan has asked my hand in marriage, father.

THE COMMANDER. Might not I perhaps eventually have a few words to say on that subject?

DON JUAN. I had intended to come to speak to you of it, Señor.

THE COMMANDER. You should have begun with that. It is precisely about a marriage proposal that I came to see you, daughter. As for you, Señor, you will understand that I cannot answer to a proposition about which no one has consulted me. All that I can say is that it would please me greatly if you would leave this house

123

as soon as possible and never set foot in it again. I will see to it
that you keep your distance.

ANNE. Father, please.

DON JUAN. My love must be great to pardon you these words. (*a
pause*) I have the honor of asking for your daughter's hand,
Señor.

THE COMMANDER. You will not have it! Please leave this room!

Don Juan turns his back on him and addresses Anne.

DON JUAN. I have the honor of asking your hand in marriage, Anne.

A long pause.

ANNE. (*softly*) Granted.

THE COMMANDER. (*shouting*) Anne de Ulloa!

DON JUAN. (*bowing deeply to Anne*) Au revoir, Anne. (*Turning toward the Commander*) Farewell, Señor. I shall come soon to seek
my fiancée. (*He leaves*)

Scene IV

THE COMMANDER. Have you completely forgotten all the respect
that you owe me, Anne de Ulloa? You will never see this man
again in your life.

ANNE. I beg you to forgive me, father. But you cannot untie what
God has tied. I love Don Juan. He loves me. Nothing can prevent
my belonging to him one day with all my body, as I now belong
to him with all my soul.

THE COMMANDER. You will not see him again, I say. Must I chain
you up and keep watch over you night and day? Besides, I have
found a husband for you.

ANNE. Father, you know that I have complied with all your wishes.
I have always obeyed you in everything — with patience and joy.
Because I respect and love you. But this time neither your will nor
my respect can influence the situation. For my love goes beyond
your person and mine. One has no power over what comes from
heaven.

THE COMMANDER. Anne de Ulloa, Don Manuel La Mota has done

me the honor of asking for your hand. I told him that I would consult you because I still thought you wise enough to choose for yourself the man who would become your husband. It seems that I was mistaken. I am therefore going to tell him that you accept. He will be your husband.

ANNE. He will not, father, even if you drag me before the priest.

THE COMMANDER. I give you a choice: either you accept him today or you enter a convent tomorrow.

ANNE. I would choose death if need be, father. And death would be life beside the union that you propose to me.

A pause.

THE COMMANDER. Yesterday you were still a little girl, Anne. What spell has this man cast over you?

ANNE. Father, what spell did you cast over my mother? At my age, she was your wife. Perhaps she too had to struggle to have the man she wanted?

THE COMMANDER. I was not the seducer of married women nor the ravisher of nuns.

ANNE. Juan was those things. He is no longer. And it is my work to have turned him away from evil. And perhaps because of that I love him.

THE COMMANDER. He would make you unhappy. You do not know him.

ANNE. What would happen to me with a man who would be nothing to me? (*She kneels down*) Father, I beg you to let me live.

THE COMMANDER. It's useless to insist, Anne. Get up! You will see Don Manuel. He'll perhaps be able to persuade you.

ANNE. (*who has got up*) Father! . . . Will he also make me believe that this table is a vase and that it is dark in plain daylight?

THE COMMANDER. How do you dare mock me like this?

ANNE. God forbid that I do, father. But, believe me, I . . .

THE COMMANDER. It is not dark in plain daylight, but the walls of this room may become those of a cloistered cell if you do not listen to reason. Enough for now; I have exhausted my patience. Farewell. (*He leaves*)

Scene V

ANNE. (*She kneels in front of the crucifix in the part of the room reserved for the oratory*) Lord, forgive me for resisting my father. But I know that by resisting him, I am obeying your designs. He says that my love is unworthy. How can he judge, Lord, the countenance that you have chosen for me? Lord, grant me the courage to fight to the end for this faith that you have given me. I have sought you for a long time in pride and solitude. Now that you have appeared to me, I bless the trials that you have me undergo. Bless my love that it may triumph over them. I believed it too great for my heart. But what would love be were it not too great? I thought it too heavy for my shoulders. But what would the cross be were it not too heavy? Thank you, oh Lord, for having let me endure this passion of joy! Test me, oh Lord. The harder the struggle the greater will be the love. Amen!
She rises. Isabella has entered on her final words.

Scene VI

ANNE. You, Señora?

ISABELLA. You are surprised to see me. I came in and didn't see anyone. (*a pause*) Juan has been here?

ANNE. Yes.

ISABELLA. He just told me so. He said good-bye, did he?

ANNE. We said au revoir.

ISABELLA. Until the happy day when you are reunited?

ANNE. Until that happy day, yes.

ISABELLA. You really believe that?

ANNE. Yes. We really believe that. Both of us. (*Isabella smiles or pretends to smile. A pause*) What can I do for you, Señora?

ISABELLA. Nothing. I have simply come to say good-bye.

ANNE. You are leaving Seville?

ISABELLA. (*pretending to be astonished*) You did not know? I am leaving for Sicily.

ANNE. You are leaving for Sicily? With him?

126

ISABELLA. Yes, of course.

ANNE. It is not true!

A pause.

ISABELLA. And why, if you please, would it not be true?

ANNE. He told me that he would not take you with him.

ISABELLA. He has since changed his mind.

ANNE. That is not possible! It isn't true. He loves me.

ISABELLA. He told you so, I'm sure.

ANNE. Yes. And he was sincere.

ISABELLA. I believe you. He told me the same thing not long ago. And he was sincere, too. Juan is always sincere when he is lying: his sincerity offers no other difficulty than that of frequently changing its object.

ANNE. He does not love you. He will not leave with you.

ISABELLA. Since when, Señorita, does Don Juan need to love a woman to be her lover and to take her with him?

ANNE. You are right. (*a short pause*) It's by depriving himself of being her lover that he learns to love her. He has not been mine.

ISABELLA. Is that his fault?

ANNE. If he wanted to be just slightly, if he urged me just slightly, how quickly I would run to him.

ISABELLA. (*mockingly*) And he does not give you that little signal?

ANNE. No, for the first time, he is patient, because for the first time he wants something other than just a body.

ISABELLA. Or because he does not wish this particular body. A man who has lived to the hilt can at certain times find distraction in a platonic friendship. To call that love seems to me very daring. That patience, as you call it, costs him very little. I presume that you are not unaware that I furnish him . . . all the compensations that he may desire.

ANNE. You lie. You are no longer anything to him. You won't shake me in the slightest.

ISABELLA. Far be it from me to think of doing so, Señorita. Your purity is a gift that is all too precious . . .

ANNE. You won't deceive me either. I have now understood you. Do you want me to tell you what your dearest wish is? You would like Don Juan to become my lover. I would be less dangerous, wouldn't I? That would be like the other times, wouldn't it? You would adjust yourself perfectly to one more infidelity, since in the end he has always come back to you. But this is more serious: I am not even his mistress. How can one fight what does not exist?

ISABELLA. You are not without imagination, Señorita!

ANNE. I defend my rights, as you defend what you believe to be yours. If you could see me in his arms, conquered like the others, subdued like the others, what a beautiful triumph that would be for you, would it not? I would have become again the anonymous prey! A simple distraction for Don Juan. Not even an infidelity. You would keep your scepter. Yes, it would be my loss. But it would also be his. I am his last chance, you understand, his last chance to be saved.

ISABELLA. You are not lacking in pretension, either.

ANNE. Resign yourself to the fact, Señora, that your reign is over.

ISABELLA. And that yours is beginning, you think? I still have some good weapons.

ANNE. His weakness and his vice. Those were, in fact, good weapons. But their time has passed. He gives me what he has never given you: unconditional love.

ISABELLA. You little fool! There is no such thing as unconditional love. You imagine that he loves you. And I grant you that he also imagines it for the moment. Because you leave him thirsting. Don't you feel how artificial this all is? When you are his mistress, you will know if he loves you. Only then can you really laugh or weep. He will then be either attached or free. In the meantime you are both involved in a silly game. Because you are afraid!

ANNE. I am not afraid. I shall be his wife.

ISABELLA. Ah, yes! The chains! You call that unconditional love.

ANNE. I shall be his wife. We'll have a long, long life together. The same joys, the same agonies . . .

ISABELLA. The same bed?

ANNE. The same bed.

ISABELLA. He may not be there every night.

ANNE. He will be there every night. The same skies, the same journeys, the same lamp, the same bread. (*Isabella bursts into painful laughter*) And one day I shall bear him children.

ISABELLA. And when you are both old, you will go sit on the same bench, under the same sun, and exchange the same memories of your sweet past love. You really believe in all that?

ANNE. I believe in it, as I believe in God.

ISABELLA. The time of tears will come one day.

ANNE. Until then, you may weep your own.

ISABELLA. My turn to laugh will come, too.

ANNE. You are mad with jealousy. I am sure now that he is not taking you with him.

ISABELLA. I am leaving all the same. I shall take the same road that he takes, step by step, behind him, without his noticing me. I shall be on the lookout for each of his failures, each of his weaknesses, each of his desires. I shall follow him tirelessly.

ANNE. Like a bitch . . .

ISABELLA. If you like. It will be my turn to be patient. I know Don Juan better than you, little girl. I don't know if you are capable of understanding me, but physical desire in him takes unexpected turns.

ANNE. A bitch. You are a bitch.

ISABELLA. I shall follow my master faithfully. Step by step, I tell you. If you like, I shall send you a letter the day he is again in my arms.

ANNE. He will never again be there. He is no longer made for the kind of love you can give him.

ISABELLA. I can give him all kinds of love. I have given him all of love. Little idiot, I give him more in one second than you can give him in the whole of your life. It is in proportion to my love that I exist. If I had loved him less, I would not have existed. He has had all of me. It is because I have loved him that I have not had your beautiful patience. I had nothing but my thirst. I counted nothing. I measured nothing. I hurled myself at him, as one who is being asphyxiated hurls himself into the air.

ANNE. (*taking a step toward Isabella*) Go.

ISABELLA. (*taking a step back toward the door*) I will get him back.

129

ANNE. (*advancing still*) Go. Get out.

ISABELLA. (*still recoiling*) He will always return to me.

ANNE. (*advancing more and more*) Get out.

ISABELLA. (*from the doorway*) Three months in Sicily. The nights there are long and beautiful.

ANNE. (*screaming*) Get out!

Isabella leaves. Mamita enters.

Scene VII

MAMITA. What have you done, my darling? Your father is terribly angry. I learned from one of the palace guards that he gave orders to pursue Don Juan and arrest him. The men are about to leave, if they are not already on their way. Don Manuel La Mota, who was once his friend, swears that he will kill him if he meets him.

ANNE. You must reach him before they do. Run and warn him. Tell him to hide.

MAMITA. He won't. You know how proud he is.

ANNE. Tell him to hide, for the sake of his love for me.

MAMITA. Yes.

ANNE. Hurry. (*As Mamita starts to leave, Anne calls her back*) Wait. (*She hesitates for a few seconds*) Tell him that if he wants to see me again before he leaves, he may come at two in the morning to the palace. Tell him to come through the little door into the garden. You will explain to him where it is. It will be open. Tell him to hide from now until then. Tell him that if he lets himself be taken, he will not see me.

MAMITA. You want to allow a man in here tonight?

ANNE. That is the only way to be sure that he will hide until then. Go quickly. Each second is precious.

MAMITA. I will not do that errand for you, my sweet. I cannot. What would your mother think if she were still alive?

ANNE. She would understand me. Go quickly. Do you want me to throw myself out the window right now before your very eyes? I swear that I will if you don't leave at once. (*She goes to the win-*

dow. Mamita hesitates) Be quick. The guards have perhaps already left.

MAMITA. (*still hesitating*) My little girl is about to become a woman without honor.

ANNE. My honor is to love the man I love in the way I love him. Go now.

Won over, Mamita leaves. Anne stands a few moments motionless at the center of the stage.

CURTAIN

SECOND TABLEAU

The same setting. Night of the same day. The window is open on the darkness. A few candles. The brass lamp is lit.

Scene I

ANNE. Almost time, Mamita. Did you explain to him carefully where the little door was?

MAMITA. Yes . . .

ANNE. Tell me all that he told you.

MAMITA. He did not want to hide. But when he learned that you would wait for him tonight to say farewell . . .

ANNE. Did he seem happy?

MAMITA. He was quiet for some time and looked at me without seeming to see me. Then he spoke slowly: "Tell your mistress that her will will be done." Those were his exact words.

ANNE. And didn't he seem happy at the thought of seeing me again?

MAMITA. I don't know. One would have thought that he expected it. But you've had me go over that now ten times. Have you lost your mind?

ANNE. Yes, Mamita. I have lost everything. I have forgotten everything, except for one thing: he is coming. He will be here soon. And I shall see him once more.

MAMITA. If your father knew that . . .

ANNE. He won't know, Mamita. You won't tell him, will you? Nor will I. No one will tell him. It will be a secret between us and the night. (*She has gone to the window*) How beautiful the night is. I have the impression of really seeing it for the first time. It is as blue as the sea, and filled with stars. It trembles like me, waiting for my beloved.

MAMITA. Night is the cape of Don Juan.

ANNE. Ah, be quiet, Mamita. Don Juan exists no more. There is only my beloved, whose love is as virgin as my body.

MAMITA. Your body won't be that much longer.

ANNE. What are you thinking, Mamita? I want simply to say goodbye to him. Is that what he thinks, too? I understand now. But he will not touch me. I don't want him to touch me.

MAMITA. You don't want him to? Come now, you are dying to have him do it.

ANNE. What is the matter with you, Mamita? Why talk to me in this way? What have I done?

MAMITA. Oh, nothing. You have changed . . . You are no longer the little girl I loved. You are someone else. You are a woman waiting for her lover.

A pause.

ANNE. One day life arrives, Mamita. The little girl wakes up one morning and discovers her soul has changed. Everything around her has a different sound, a different color. Everything is fresh in the world, trees and brooks, skies and dreams. And she, too, is completely fresh, smooth, washed clean of her little past. I am not responsible, Mamita, if life has assumed this face. (*a pause*) I am under his power. I cannot be touched by anything that does not come from him.

MAMITA. (*who has been gazing out the window*) Be calm. He is coming. He must not see you like this.

ANNE. But I am very calm, Mamita . . .

132

A minute or two later, Don Juan enters. He throws his cape down on a chair. Mamita goes out.

Scene II

ANNE. (*running to him*) How long the day has been, Juan.

DON JUAN. Nothing could happen to me with you waiting for me.

ANNE. I am so afraid of this journey . . .

DON JUAN. Do you want me to stay?

ANNE. You know very well that is impossible. My father would have you arrested . . .

DON JUAN. Will you leave with me?

A pause.

ANNE. I cannot, Juan, I must stay here and struggle for you. Will you have the strength to wait for me?

DON JUAN. This is the second time today you've asked me that. I have promised you.

ANNE. It is just that Isabella came a little while ago.

DON JUAN. What did she say?

ANNE. That she would win you back in the end.

DON JUAN. Isabella is mad.

ANNE. She, too, loves you, Juan. A woman in love is dangerous.

DON JUAN. Are you afraid of her?

ANNE. No. (*a short pause*) I think I would have hated a man who brought me only security. With you, my happiness will go from danger to danger. But what would happiness be without each new threat? You are full of life, Juan, and you give life to me. (*a pause*) Why are you smiling?

DON JUAN. I don't know, Anne, I look at you and I am happy. Who would have thought that happiness would come to me from a little girl?

ANNE. I am no longer a little girl, Juan. I astonished my father and Mamita just now; they no longer recognized me. (*She raises herself up on her heels*) Haven't I grown in the last few weeks?

DON JUAN. (*very gravely*) Yes, Anne, you have grown.

ANNE. Smile again, Juan.

133

DON JUAN. Like that? (*He smiles*)

ANNE. Yes. You have a childlike smile. I have never really seen you smile. Only seen you laugh, with a laugh that chilled me through. No, Juan, I am no longer a little girl. It is you who have become a little boy again.

DON JUAN. Yes, Anne.

ANNE. I am very old.

DON JUAN. Yes, Anne. You must teach me what life is all about.

ANNE. I shall teach you. I shall teach you about women too. I shall be all women to you: in turn wise and silly, cold and tender, sad and gay, candid and perverse, queen and servant.

DON JUAN. And how shall I be able to recognize your real face in all that?

ANNE. All my faces will be real, since under all these aspects, I shall love you.

DON JUAN. And what shall I do? What soul shall I assume?

ANNE. Your own is sufficient, my darling. I'm even afraid that all the faces I may adopt won't succeed in satisfying it. (*A pause. Suddenly changing her tone*) I'm afraid suddenly. Tell me, Juan, that everything will not be destroyed, that everything will not be lost, that we will not be unworthy. That neither of us will be unworthy of what he holds at this moment in his hands and which has become life? Swear to me, Juan.

DON JUAN. I swear, Anne. Nothing but you will exist for me.

ANNE. (*regaining confidence quite quickly*) No, nothing, Juan. It is easy, really. All we need is enough love.

DON JUAN. Yes, my darling. All we need is enough love. How light everything becomes around you. How simple everything becomes. Unbelievably simple. Absolute security. You were saying just now that you would hate a man who would bring you only that. I think you will hate me, Anne . . . For you will have nothing to struggle against, my little warrior, my miniature Minerva, my little St. George. No dragons to slay with those tough little hands. Not even a wolf. You will see how monotonous it is to be so peaceful. Who knows? Perhaps you'll be the one who will want to deceive me?

ANNE. (*smiling also*) Who knows, Juan?

DON JUAN. How shall we spend our evenings? Will you make music for me?

ANNE. Yes, Juan.

DON JUAN. Will you dance for me?

ANNE. Yes, Juan.

DON JUAN. Will we throw dice together?

ANNE. Yes, Juan.

DON JUAN. Will you tell me fairy tales about ogres and naughty fairies?

ANNE. Yes, Juan. But you will have to rock me slowly to sleep.

DON JUAN. I will, and I'll sing you — off key, of course — some of those tearful songs in which a lover has gone forever or love is unrequited. (*He hums*)

> When the prince went off to war,
> He wept as he kissed his love.
> With my body afar, and my love here,
> Keep my heart in heaven above.

ANNE. How happy your face is, Juan.

DON JUAN. You can see that I am nothing but a little boy.

A long pause.

ANNE. When will your ship leave?

DON JUAN. One hour before dawn. The time is approaching.

A long pause.

ANNE. The weeks will be long.

DON JUAN. Yes.

ANNE. As long as death.

DON JUAN. Yes.

A long pause.

ANNE. Will you kiss me, Juan? (*They both hesitate a moment, then throw themselves into each others' arms. She tears herself away some time later and falls into a chair weeping, her face in her hands. He approaches her, kneels down, and strokes her hair very slowly and tenderly*) How weak and cowardly I am, Juan! How cowardly I am!

135

DON JUAN. No, my sweet, no.

ANNE. I had hoped for so much. Now it's all over.

DON JUAN. No, my sweet, no.

ANNE. I thought I could endure this waiting. I had armed myself with all my poor patience. I had hoped to resist the force that drew me toward you, I had hoped not to hear that voice that was screaming within me. I had hoped, Juan. I had strained all my strength to hold out until that giddy day when I could call you my husband. Now I know that I shall feel no more peace until I am again in your arms. Forgive me, Juan. It is clear that I shall be just like all the other women you have known.

DON JUAN. No, my sweet, no. I love you.

She spreads her hands, looks at him through her tears, and attempts a courageous little smile.

ANNE. In spite of everything, Juan?

DON JUAN. In spite of everything, Anne. I love you. You love me. I'm going to leave. The crew is already on board the ship that is to take me away. They are at their posts. Can you hear the officers shout their orders as they look up at the masts? Soon the sails will stretch before the wind. Can you hear the anchor chain being raised, and the water dripping from it? Can you hear, Anne? Do you hear the scraping of the iron hanks and the gentle sound of the rain that accompanies the shifting of the sails? Can you hear, Anne?

ANNE. Juan, ah, Juan, be quiet.

DON JUAN. (*pitilessly*) I shall soon be on that ship. We shall drop the last line, take up the last gangplank. And the ship will leave the quay and begin to sail down the river.

ANNE. Juan, be quiet.

DON JUAN. (*in the same tone of voice*) I shall be leaning on the rail aft. It will be cold. And I shall watch in the distance the lights of Seville sink slowly down. Then I shall see nothing but the riverbanks in the half-light of dawn. When we reach the sea, it will be midday. (*Don Juan has now got up again. He stands very straight and looks through the window toward a horizon one cannot see*)

136

ANNE. Juan, Juan, what is the matter with you?

DON JUAN. I'm simply living these last minutes together, Anne. Living them to the full, as would a dying man.

ANNE. (*crying out*) Juan, you don't love me any more.

DON JUAN. You will be mine now, Anne.

ANNE. (*drawing back, her voice suddenly filled with terror*) No. No.

DON JUAN. You will be mine. What good was all this patience?

ANNE. No, Juan. No.

DON JUAN. Such is life. We have for a while cherished a mad illusion. I desire your body, Anne. Isn't that also love?

ANNE. That will be the end, Juan . . .

DON JUAN. But no.

ANNE. (*almost in tears*) That will be the end . . . for you and me. All that came before us and did not yet have a name. All that we had to build through faith and dream. All that we have not yet earned. This folly, this sweetness. (*He approaches her with determination. She draws back*) No, Juan, I beg you. Not yet. Not tonight. Leave now.

He continues to approach her.

DON JUAN. I won't rest until you are mine, Anne.

ANNE. (*weakening*) No . . . no. (*He takes her in his arms and tries to embrace her. She resists, then yields*) We are lost . . .

DON JUAN. Why? It is just the beginning. (*He lifts her in his arms*)

ANNE. All is over.

He carries her into the bedroom. The stage is empty. A long pause. Then may be heard, coming from the street, the muffled sound of a bell and the voice of the watchman announcing the time.

VOICE OF THE WATCHMAN. Three A.M. All is calm. Tomorrow, fair and warm. Good people, sleep well.

One second more, the stage still empty, then the door of the hallway opens. Mamita timidly puts her head in, sees no one, then enters. She immediately looks in the direction of Anne's bedroom and gestures sadly. At this moment, the Commander enters. Mamita sees him and draws back in fright, screaming: Good Lord!

137

Scene III

THE COMMANDER. What does all this mean? Why have you kept the light on? What are you doing here?

MAMITA. (*gulping*) I . . . I couldn't sleep, Master. I got up and prayed for a while.

THE COMMANDER. Where is my daughter?

MAMITA. Anne? She's asleep by this time, I suppose . . . The poor angel. I think . . . I think I'm going to try to get some rest too. (*She tries to guide the Commander to the door*) May I put out the lights, Master?

THE COMMANDER. (*after a pause*) Yes. (*Mamita blows out a candle and starts to blow out another, when the Commander notices the cape that Don Juan has left*) Wait! What is this?

MAMITA. (*upset*) I don't know, Master. It's probably the cloak of the gentleman who came a while ago; he must have forgotten it . . .

THE COMMANDER. He must have forgotten . . . (*He stands for a moment motionless holding the cape in his hands. Then he goes rapidly toward the door of Anne's bedroom*)

MAMITA. (*screaming*) No!

The Commander pushes her brutally aside and enters. Mamita falls on her knees and clasps her hands in prayer. Long, very long minutes pass. Then a cry. And the Commander, holding his side in his two hands, leaves the room, staggers a short way, and falls dead in the center of the stage. Don Juan appears in turn on the threshold of Anne's room, sword drawn, very straight, motionless. Anne rushes out past him, and throws herself on her father's body. Mamita is still on her knees praying; her voice may be heard rising gradually between Anne's sobs and Don Juan's silence.

Scene IV

MAMITA. . . . Do not let me burn in hell fire. I pray to you, prostrate and suppliant, my heart crushed to cinders; care for me at the hour of my death. Oh, day of tears when the guilty man will rise up from the dust of the tomb to be judged. Forgive him, oh Lord. Lord, gentle Jesus, give him rest. Amen . . .

Mamita's voice dies out while Don Juan slowly approaches Anne, who is still prostrate.

DON JUAN. (*gently*) Anne . . . (*Anne's sobs quiet down. She does not move any longer*) Anne . . . (*She gets up slowly*) Farewell, Anne. Call your people.

A long pause. Anne looks at Don Juan and passes her hand across her forehead as if she were waking up.

ANNE. Go, Juan. Your ship is ready to sail.

DON JUAN. Why leave, Anne, if I am forbidden to see you again? It's better that they take me.

ANNE. Leave. Before the Supreme Judge we shall bear the weight of this crime. And we shall share it in His eyes through all eternity, just as I had hoped we would share our bread. But we need not answer for it in the eyes of men. Their cells and their chains are nothing beside what awaits us. Go!

DON JUAN. I shall obey you, Anne. But if there is a God, He cannot prevent me from bearing the full responsibility for all this. (*a pause*) What are you going to do?

ANNE. I shall enter a convent tomorrow. If tears can wash away transgression, one day there will be no trace of mine. Farewell, Juan! God knows that I loved you. But in the world you enter now, nothing can save you. Not even my prayers. Go.

A long pause.

DON JUAN. I was born to destroy. Farewell, Anne.

He leaves. Anne staggers forward, leans against the wall, but manages to remain upright.

Scene V

Mamita gets up and starts to leave to shout for help.

ANNE. (*very weary*) Be quiet and stay here.

MAMITA. But I must call someone. You can't leave your father like this.

139

ANNE. We can no longer do anything for him. He is with God. (*Mamita gestures again toward the door*) Wait, I say.

MAMITA. Wait for what? You have done enough mad things.

ANNE. Wait until Don Juan is far away.

MAMITA. He will burn in eternal flame.

Anne, without answering, goes toward the crucifix and prays in silence. A long pause. Then she rises, still very slowly.

ANNE. You may call the people now.

MAMITA. (*opens the door and leaves screaming*) Help, help, the Commander has been killed. Help, help! . . .

Her cries may be heard echoing down the corridors of the palace. Anne remains alone on the stage, motionless and rigid. She looks toward the window where day is slowly breaking.

CURTAIN